Don't Get Taken!

DON'T GET TAKEN!

How to Avoid Everyday Consumer Rip-offs

STEVEN MITCHELL SACK

and the Editors of

Consumer Reports Books

CONSUMER REPORTS BOOKS

A Division of Consumers Union

Yonkers, New York

Library of Congress Cataloging-in-Publication Data

Sack, Steven Mitchell, 1954–
    Don't get taken! : how to avoid everyday consumer rip-offs / by
Steven Mitchell Sack and the editors of Consumer Reports Books.
     p.   cm.
    Includes index.
    ISBN 0-89043-442-0 (pbk.)
    1.   Consumer protection—Law and legislation—United States—
Popular works.   2. Labor laws and legislation—United States—
Popular works.   I. Consumer Reports Books. II. Title.
KF1610.S23 1993
343.73'071—dc20
[347.30371]
             92-34507
             CIP

Design by Joy Taylor

First printing, February 1993

Manufactured in the United States of America

Contents

Acknowledgments

Generous thanks are extended to my editor, Roslyn Siegel, at Consumer Reports Books. Roslyn's patience, vision, intuition, and confidence in this project were invaluable; without her, this book would not have been written.

I also wish to thank Gabrielle Vitellio, Esq., for her capable research skills. Acknowledgments are also extended to my brother and New York City law partner Jonathan Scott Sack, Esq., who provided me with several rough drafts of text that were eventually incorporated into the book and whose friendship and loyalty are always appreciated.

Special thanks are given to Subhash Gulati, M.D., who literally saved my life and enabled me to continue my work.

As always, I wish to express my appreciation and gratitude to Joan and Sidney Pollack; and to my mother, Judith, and my father, Bernard, whose vision of providing practical, preventive legal strategies to people in all phases of life was instilled in me at an early age and who dreamed that one day I would write a book for the consumer. Finally, thoughts of love go to my wife, Gwen, and son, Andrew, for future dreams.

Introduction

Most consumers know very little about the way the law affects their lives. But without this knowledge, you can be financially exploited. As a practicing lawyer, I see the mistakes people make—entering into deals without investigating the facts; making expensive purchases without reading or understanding the fine print; and worst, failing to take simple steps to protect their rights. The consequences of these acts are often very costly. Problems can, however, usually be avoided if you know what to do.

This book contains practical strategies for many of the consumer decisions you are faced with. Whatever your background, education, and experience, you can learn how to detect problems before they occur and be aware of the legal consequences of your acts. Much of this information can be implemented without a lawyer. And even if litigation becomes necessary, your chances of success increase substantially when you have recognized the problem and documented your claim.

Many of the items discussed encompass simple rules of common sense and reason. When you are making an expensive purchase or hiring an architect, there is no limit to the kinds of provisions that can be negotiated and inserted into the purchase agreement or contract. Imaginative use of written agreements can result in significant protections and savings.

To be adequately protected, consumers must apply the principles of "preventive law" in all their dealings. Maintain careful records of your transactions, send letters of protest to document your dissatisfaction whenever problems arise, and take proper steps without delay to enforce your rights where warranted. You can help enhance your legal position whether you decide to settle a dispute or litigate, provided you act promptly and properly.

By using this book as your guide and learning the applicable laws in your state, you can minimize potential areas of conflict. There is a large body of consumer law created to further fairness and justice. It is there to protect you, so know the law and enforce your rights.

An informed consumer always:

- asks questions
- reads the fine print
- investigates credentials and checks references
- gets the terms of the deal in writing
- sends a letter or agreement confirming the deal if none is received
- keeps careful records
- protests unfair or illegal treatment
- follows up with stronger action if satisfaction is not received
- researches applicable law and consults an attorney immediately when necessary
- knows his or her rights

Using this book as your guide, you can avoid problems in many common consumer transactions and enforce your rights if problems arise.

Steven Mitchell Sack
Attorney-at-Law
New York, N.Y.

Don't Get Taken!

Protecting Your Income

Exercising Your Rights in the Workplace

Traditionally, the law favored employers when it came to resolving employment disputes. Most people could be fired at whim, without cause or notice, and bosses had little fear of legal reprisal. Now, however, the law provides workers with more protection. Since more than 70 million Americans work without written contracts and basic job security, it is important to know your rights in all phases of the employment relationship—before being hired, while working for the company, and after you are fired—to take advantage of the many laws favoring employees.

PREHIRING ABUSES

The Hiring Procedure

If you are hired properly, you can increase your job security, compensation package, and other benefits. Many people accept work without clearly defining the terms of their employment. Others forget to ask for a written contract. They shake hands with their new employer and assume that everything will go smoothly. When misunderstandings develop, they are at a significant disadvantage.

Investigate potential employers. Find out all you can about a business's reputation, financial status, and credit rating, and how it treats its employees. For example, if you are being hired to replace someone, try to learn the name of that person and the reason he or she is no longer there. If possible, speak to the person. Investigate an employer's credit rating to discover if the business is having financial difficulties. Such information can often be obtained from a credit-reporting agency or bank. The following are significant items worth investigating:

- Does the employer conduct business as a corporation, Subchapter S corporation, partnership, or sole proprietorship?
- What are the names of the principal shareholders or partners?
- How many people does the business employ?
- What are the locations and kinds of real property and other assets owned by the employer?
- Does the employer have a history of litigation, and are there any outstanding encumbrances or liens?
- Was the business sold recently, and did the new owners assume its liabilities or just purchase the assets?

Investigate the status of the person hiring you. Employers sometimes argue in court that an employee was hired by someone who did not have the authority to offer employment, negotiate compensation, or live up to the agreed-upon terms. Only an officer (such as a vice president) or owner can bind the company. Make sure the person hiring you has such authority.

Recognize illegal employment inquiries. It is illegal to ask certain questions on employment applications or during hiring interviews. For example, inquiries pertaining to arrest records or drug use are illegal because employers are supposed to consider you as you now are and not as you have been in the past. Female applicants are often asked about marriage plans (Do you plan on getting married soon and raising a family?). Some employers avoid liability by asking applicants to sign documents called "waivers," which give the employer permission to acquire information about your credit rating, medical history, and arrest record. Inquiries about an applicant's race, color, age, gender, sexual preference, religion, and national origin are illegal.

Inquiries about an applicant's race, color, age, gender, sexual preference, religion, or national origin are illegal.

The use of polygraph or lie detector exams by private employers has become the subject of increased scrutiny and criticism. The federal Polygraph Protection Act of 1988 was enacted to curb many abuses. The law now *forbids* the use of such tests for any job applicant.

Many states have also enacted strong laws protecting job applicants from stress tests, psychological evaluator tests, and other honesty tests. In some states the trend is to eliminate or strongly discourage the use of such tests. Therefore, before submitting to any such test, research the current status of the law in your state.

Finally, recognize that employers sometimes violate the law when testing the basic skills levels of job applicants (called "skills tests"). Since the failure to pass such tests could be viewed as the result of an attempt to exclude certain groups on the basis of race, age, sex, national origin, or religion, employers must be very careful. Under guidelines adopted by the Equal Employment Opportunity Commission (EEOC), all literacy tests for prospective employees must be job-related and adequately evaluate the applicant's ability to perform the duties and tasks of the job involved.

The laws about legal and illegal inquiries are complicated. For example, although it may be illegal to ask you to fill out a medical history form, an employer can ask you to submit to a preemployment physical, provided all applicants are required to take these physicals as the last part of the screening process and being fit is essential for job performance (i.e., a fire fighter). However, it is illegal for doctors to ask discriminatory questions—for example, regarding the amount of time taken off for illness in the past two years or whether you have ever been compensated for an injury—during the examination.

Similarly, employers are allowed to conduct a credit check of an applicant if this serves a legitimate business purpose. However, the Fair Credit Reporting Act restricts employers from using consumer credit reports for employment decisions (such as granting promotions). If the employer orders a report, you must be told and given the name and address of the credit agency that is supplying it.

It is legal for an employer to ask your age and marital status *after* you start working in order to compute pension and other compensation benefits. But your answers cannot be used to make promotion, transfer, or firing decisions, and such questions must be asked of all employees in the organization.

Answering illegal inquiries. It is sometimes difficult to avoid answering an illegal question without appearing hostile or conveying the impression you have something to hide. You might disarm the interviewer by asking the significance of the question and then choosing not to answer it on the basis of irrelevance.

Know the law. To learn if you have been victimized by an illegal hiring practice, check the laws in your state. Many states have detailed guidelines on preemployment inquiries.

If you believe you were denied a job after answering an illegal question, contact a regional office of the Civil Liberties Union, Human Rights Commission, or Equal Employment Opportunity Commission. It is best to send a letter to document your claim (see Figure 1.1). After sending the letter, contact the agency to determine the course of action to take. It may also be appropriate to speak to a lawyer.

Recognize unusual legal conditions of employment. In some states, employers can fingerprint and photograph applicants as a condition of employment. The federal government may require you to be fingerprinted if you apply for a civil service job. However, you cannot be denied a job if you refuse to be fingerprinted and the law in your state prohibits this. You may also be required to live in the village or county where you work. So-called residence statutes have been declared constitutional by the U.S. Supreme Court. This is particularly true if you accept a civil service job.

Avoid being victimized by job misrepresentation. There are many phony advertisements promising substantial income for part-time work or offering employment with unlimited earning potential. A typical ad looks like this:

> **BE YOUR OWN BOSS by working at home.**
> **No experience necessary.**
> **Over $500 per week possible.**

If a job sounds too good to be true, it probably is. Unfortunately, most people learn the ads are misleading only after they have been exploited.

Making the purchase of goods a condition of employment may be illegal. To protect yourself against these and other schemes, take the following precautions:

- Be wary of guaranteed earnings claims. You have the right to know the facts. For example, if you are promised a certain sum because

George, interested in a sales career, was attracted by an ad stating that a company was looking for an aggressive individual to sell its product. Experience was not required because the company used national advertising and a dedicated staff to assist its employees. The ad promised substantial income immediately. George contacted the company and traveled at his own expense to meet the potential employer. There he discovered the catch: It was necessary to buy $5,000 worth of the product in order to sell it!

this is what other employees make, ask the employer to authenticate the claim. According to the Federal Trade Commission (FTC), it is an unfair and deceptive trade practice to promise you an amount that exceeds the average net earnings of other employees.

- Know what assistance you will receive. Some employers exaggerate the amount and quality of help to be rendered. Speak to the people who will supposedly assist you.
- Refuse job offers that make you buy before you work.
- Beware of work-at-home employment ads. Many such ads are illegal.

Protecting your rights. If you have been victimized by an employment scheme or work-at-home advertisement, do the following immediately:

1. Call the regional office of the Federal Trade Commission. The FTC can investigate on your behalf and impose a cease-and-desist order on the company to discontinue illegal practices.
2. Inform your employer you are taking action. Tell him or her you will file a complaint with the FTC if you are not reimbursed for your losses. Many employers are reluctant to tangle with the FTC and are inclined to settle matters amicably.
3. Contact your local Better Business Bureau (BBB). The BBB cannot impose sanctions the way the FTC can, but it can pressure a business to correct complaints. The BBB maintains a national list

> *A study by the Council of Better Business Bureaus examined one kind of work-at-home ad—envelope stuffing—to determine if it was misleading. The ads guaranteed earnings of up to $1,000 per week. The council concluded that people were spending more money to purchase introductory mailing lists than they could possibly earn back.*

of individuals and companies that have been accused of engaging in misleading advertising and improper business practices. You can obtain this information by asking for it.

4. Contact the Postal Service. The Postal Service can ask employers to voluntarily halt illegal practices. It can also issue federal court orders that prevent businesses from receiving mail.

5. Speak to a lawyer. Some state laws protect victims of misleading trade practices and employment schemes. A statute such as the Uniform Deceptive Trade Practices Act may have been passed in your state. This allows a person to be represented by the state attorney general's office (which can sue for damages and equitable relief on your behalf).

Discuss key employment terms. No matter what type of job you accept, it is critical to discuss all the terms and conditions of employment before you agree to work. The following are important points to consider:

- On what date is your employment to begin?
- What is the length of employment: Are you employed for a definite term or are you employed at will? If employed for a definite term, is the contract renewable? Can one or both parties terminate employment prior to the expiration of the term? If so, how much notice (if any) must be given before the termination is effective?
- What is your title?
- What are your employment duties. Must you report to a superior?
- What are the number of required working hours, sick days, holidays, and vacation days?

- What is your employment status? Are you considered an employee or independent contractor? (As an independent contractor, you are required by law to pay social security, withholding taxes, and unemployment insurance.)
- What is your base salary? When is it payable? Specify all deductions from your paycheck.
- Is there a probationary period?
- Are you represented by a labor union? If so, what will your dues be?
- Are business expenses reimbursable? What, when, how, and to what extent?
- Are bonuses given? How are they calculated and when are they paid? Are prorated bonuses given if you are fired or resign prior to the natural expiration of your contract?
- Are commissions paid? If so, specify how they are earned. Is the commission based on a gross or net amount? If net, be sure you know what deductions are included.
- What are your fringe benefits? (These can include use of an automobile; free parking; car insurance; gasoline allowances; death benefits; prepaid legal services; medical, dental, and hospitalization costs; life insurance; company credit cards; keyman insurance; stock options; pension; and profit-sharing plans.) Be sure you know all the ramifications of your benefit package (such as when your pension or profit-sharing plan vests).
- Are periodic raises given? What is the procedure for merit raises and promotions?
- What happens if you become disabled? Define the meanings of temporary disability and permanent disability.
- Is a physical examination necessary?
- Will relocation be required? If so, specify who will pay for it and the manner of reimbursement.
- Can you have side ventures in a noncompeting business, or must you work exclusively on a full-time basis?
- Are you prohibited from working for a competitor after your employment ends? If so, for how long and where?
- Who owns inventions and processes created by you during employment?

Ask for a written contract. After agreeing on key employment terms, ask your employer to put these terms in writing. This will protect you in a number of ways.

- Potential misunderstandings will be reduced. Oral terms are often interpreted differently by employers and employees. Having them in writing may eliminate confusion and ambiguities for both parties.
- You decrease the chances of being fired unfairly. Working on a handshake is a risky proposition. In most states, the law says that if you are hired without a written contract, you are hired at will. This means that you can be fired at any time for any reason without advance notice.
- It is easier to prove the terms of your employment. A handshake confirms only that you accepted employment; it does not prove what was contracted for.
- Your rights may be increased. Clauses in written contracts can give you negotiating strength. For example, some employment contracts say that terms cannot be changed without the written consent of both parties. If such a clause was included in your contract and an employer attempted to reduce your salary or other benefits, this could not be done without your written approval.
- You are protected if you are fired in a manner prohibited by the contract.

No job lasts forever. Some employers promise lifetime employment yet fire employees without notice. In virtually all states, promises of employment exceeding one year are not enforceable unless they are in writing. A "lifetime contract" is probably not as secure as it sounds.

A **"lifetime contract" is not as secure as it sounds.**

Protect yourself if you cannot obtain a written contract. Ask for a fixed employment term. According to the law, when you are hired for a definite term, you cannot be fired at the boss's whim. You can be fired only for cause, such as habitual lateness; prolonged absence from work; intoxication; disrespect or unprofessional conduct; disobedience of company work rules, regulations, or policies; exceeding authority; negligence or neglect of duty; dishonesty or unfaithfulness; making secret profits;

Judith received a two-year written contract to work as a fashion designer. The contract would be automatically renewed for an additional year if notice of termination canceling the contract was not sent by September 1 of the second year. Judith was fired on December 5 of the second year, and she sued for damages. The court ruled that she was entitled to additional compensation because she was terminated improperly—the employer failed to cancel the contract by September 1 of the second year.

stealing; or misusing trade secrets, customer lists, or other confidential information.

Another way to protect yourself is to send the company a confirming letter after you are hired. Such letters of agreement must accurately reflect the terms of your employment and include any oral promises made (see Figures 1.2A and 1.2B). You should send a letter of agreement whenever you cannot obtain a written contract.

If possible, avoid signing contracts containing restrictive covenants. Restrictive covenants (also called "covenants not to compete") can prohibit you from doing many things, most commonly forming a competing venture or working for a competitor, soliciting former customers or employees, or using the knowledge acquired on the job in future endeavors.

For years, courts have struggled to balance the conflicting considerations of restrictive covenants. Some clauses are viewed as unfair because they limit a person's ability to earn a living. However, courts also recognize the legitimate interest of an employer to safeguard his or her business from deliberate commercial piracy.

Execute your contract properly. Read your contract carefully and question all ambiguous or confusing language. Contracts prepared by employers usually contain clauses that work to your disadvantage. If you are satisfied with the terms of the agreement, be sure it is signed by a bona fide representative of the company who has the authority to bind the employer to important terms. Include the date and initial all changes. If the contract refers to a schedule or additional terms contained in another document, attach that document to the contract. Obtain a signed copy of the executed agreement for your files and keep it in a safe place with other important documents.

ON-THE-JOB RIGHTS

Being properly hired is the beginning of the employment relationship. It is just as important to know what your on-the-job rights are and how to enforce them.

Privacy Rights

Your privacy rights extend to the workplace. These rights are frequently violated by executives, security personnel, private investigators, and informers. The law allows employees to recover damages under a variety of legal theories when people act improperly.

Lie detector tests. The federal Polygraph Protection Act of 1988 bans virtually all employers from requiring job applicants and regular workers (including union employees) to submit to lie detector tests. If you are pressured to take such a test, speak to a lawyer immediately.

Searches, interrogations, and access to records. Employers faced with growing security problems are resorting to stricter measures to protect company facilities, property, and employees. Although such measures accomplish their objectives, employees' rights are often violated in the process. Employers use a variety of techniques when they suspect workers of misconduct, including searching employees' offices, lockers, or homes without their knowledge or consent; requesting employees to open brief-cases or packages when leaving a company facility; and conducting a "pat-down" search of their persons.

Although each case is decided on its own merits, the law generally states that office searches are permissible if an employer has a reasonable basis for suspecting the employee of wrongdoing and the search is confined to nonpersonal areas of the employee's office. (The office and documents relevant to company business are the property of the employer.) Clearly visible personal items cannot be searched, and employers cannot conduct a search if there is no reasonable ground for suspicion. In addition, employers cannot conduct nonconsensual searches of an employee's home; doing so leaves them liable for trespass.

Searches of your briefcase, locker, or packages may be legitimate if the employer has posted signs reminding employees that personal property is subject to search. Nevertheless, the practice must be imposed on all employees. For example, searching the lockers of only one race or ethnic group of employees may be illegal.

If you believe that you are the victim of an employer's illegal search, ask yourself the following questions:

- Were similar searches conducted before?
- Were you notified that the employer reserved the right to search? If so, how?
- What was the object of the search? Was it reasonable?
- Was personal or company property confiscated?
- What did you do during the search? Who conducted the search? What were you told? By whom?
- Did you refuse to cooperate?
- Did the search have an offensive impact? Were you grabbed, jostled, or held? Were you coerced, physically threatened, or mentally abused in order to cooperate?
- Were you held against your will? Were you so intimidated by the experience that you were afraid to leave?
- Were you chosen at random with others, or were you the only one singled out and searched in front of others? If so, were you stigmatized by the suspicion of wrongdoing?

If you answered yes to some of the preceding questions, speak to a lawyer immediately. You may have a strong case for reinstatement or compensation if you were fired, placed on probation, suspended, or given an official reprimand after the search.

Access to records. Many union employees covered under collective bargaining agreements have the right to examine their own records and to be informed of what information is used in making decisions relevant to their employment. In addition, some states have passed laws allowing employees in the private sector access to their personnel records to correct incomplete or inaccurate information. Other states require employers to seek workers' approval before employee records can be collected, distributed, or destroyed. In the absence of these laws, you generally do not have the right to review your records (especially medical records, security records, and promotional schedules maintained by the employer).

It may also be illegal in your state to distribute personal information without your consent. For example, the circulation of confidential memoranda within a company has given rise to many lawsuits, particularly when the employer did not take adequate precautions to determine whether derogatory information was accurate.

> *Recently, a terminated employee sued his former boss on the basis of defamation. Letters describing the employee's poor job performance were distributed and read by several executives. The employee was awarded $90,000 after proving that company officials knew the letters were false.*

Wiretapping and eavesdropping. In most states you have the right to be told *before* a phone conversation, interview, or interrogation is taped. In addition, company lawyers have the ethical responsibility of obtaining the consent of all parties prior to recording a conversation.

Rights to unionize. The National Labor Relations Act allows employees to unionize and bargain collectively. Employers are prohibited from interfering with the exercise of these rights; they cannot fire, lay off, or demote workers who participate in such activities. In addition, an employer cannot question job applicants about their personal feelings toward unions or past activities in order to screen out potential "troublemakers." The law also protects employees who band together to protest wages, hours, or working conditions. For example, if six nonunion employees complain about inadequate air-conditioning or a smoke-filled working environment, it is likely that the employer would be prohibited from firing them as a result of their complaint. Contact your union, regional labor relations board, or state department of labor if you believe your rights have been violated.

The National Labor Relations Act allows employees to unionize and bargain collectively.

Although you cannot be forced to join a union in order to get a job, you may be required to pay periodic dues if you work in a "union shop." In a union shop, all workers eligible to join the union as well as the employer are governed by a collective-bargaining agreement, and dues are used to pay for the expenses incurred in administering this agreement. Federal employees work in an "open shop." They do not have to pay fees if they choose not to join the union, but they are still entitled to the benefits of the union contract and union representation.

Employment discrimination. Employment discrimination is illegal. Hundreds of thousands of formal complaints are currently filed with the EEOC, and more than 5,000 discrimination lawsuits are tried in court each year. The remainder are either settled out of court or dismissed for lack of proof.

Federal and state laws prohibit employers from discriminating against employees or potential employees on the basis of age, race, color, creed, religion, national origin, sex, marital status, disability, or physical handicap. Discrimination can occur during any employment stage: recruiting, interviewing, hiring, promotion, training, transfer, assignment, discipline, layoff, or discharge.

Age discrimination. Under federal law, employers can fire older workers for inadequate job performance and good cause (tardiness, intoxication, etc.); entice older workers into early retirement by offering bigger pensions, extended health insurance, substantial bonuses, and so on; lay off older workers, as long as younger employees are similarly treated; and discriminate against older applicants when successful job performance absolutely requires that a younger person be hired for the job (e.g., an air traffic controller).

However, federal law forbids private employers, labor unions, state and local government agencies, and employment agencies from:

- denying an applicant a job on the basis of age
- imposing compulsory retirement before age 70
- coercing older employees into retirement by threatening termination
- firing employees because of age
- denying promotions, transfers, or assignments because of age
- penalizing older workers with reduced privileges, employment opportunity, and compensation

Various state laws also give older workers essentially the same protection.

Damages are recoverable provided you can demonstrate that you received unfair treatment primarily because of age.

> *A 57-year-old marketing director who was fired filed a complaint with the EEOC in his state. The company defended the charges by arguing that the executive was one of 70 employees whose employment was terminated to save the company money. The company claimed there was no discrimination because the man was hired when he was 54 years old.*
>
> *The company lost the case. EEOC investigators discovered that although 70 people had been fired, 65 new employees were hired in the following year, and only four of them were over the age of 50. The executive was reinstated and awarded $48,000 in back pay, retroactive seniority, and fringe benefits.*

If you suspect you were denied a job on the basis of age, demand an explanation. Contact the EEOC if you are not satisfied with the answers given. After discussing your case with a compliance officer, the EEOC can conduct an investigation on your behalf. Your identity will be kept confidential until you decide to file formal charges.

If you believe you were fired because of your age, ask yourself the following questions:

- Did you request a transfer to another position before you were fired? Was it refused? If so, were similar requests granted to younger workers?
- How were you terminated? Were you given false reasons for the termination? Did you consent to such action or send a certified letter protesting the discharge?
- Were you replaced by a younger worker?

The answers may prove that you were fired as a result of age discrimination. Your case can be strengthened if fellow employees were also victimized.

> *An insurance company forced 143 people to retire prematurely at the age of 62. The large number of employees made it difficult for the company to overcome charges of age discrimination, and workers collectively received more than $6 million in back wages. In another case, a company denied training to two older employees and then fired them. The company claimed the men were unskilled and not qualified to continue employment. The workers filed timely claims and recovered $79,200 in lost wages, benefits, and legal fees.*

Sex discrimination. The law requires similar employment policies, standards, and practices for males and females. Equal treatment is imposed in a variety of areas, including hiring, placement, job promotion, working conditions, layoffs, and discharge. For example, it is discriminatory for an employer to refuse to hire women with preschool-age children while hiring men with children; require females to resign from jobs upon marriage when there is no similar requirement for males; include spouses of male employees in benefits plans while denying the same benefits to spouses of female employees; restrict certain jobs to men without offering a reasonable opportunity for women to demonstrate their ability to perform the same job (e.g., fire fighting); refuse to hire, train, assign, or promote pregnant or married women, or women of child-bearing age, merely on the basis of sex; deny unemployment benefits, seniority, or layoff credit to pregnant women, or deny a leave of absence for pregnancy irrespective of whether or not it is granted for illness; or institute compulsory retirement plans with lower retirement ages for women than men.

The law requires similar employment policies, standards, and practices for males and females.

A U.S. District Court judge once ordered a major airline to pay its 3,343 current and former female flight attendants $52.5 million in damages. The airline violated the Equal Pay Act by giving male attendants better pay, benefits, and working conditions than their female counterparts. At the trial, it was proved that males received more money for the same job, were given single rooms in hotels for overnight layovers (women had to double up), and were not disciplined equally after violating company "appearance" rules (women were suspended without pay if their weight was more than five pounds above company standards; men were not).

A university was ordered to pay 117 women an award of $1.3 million when a federal court special master determined that the school paid lower salaries to women on the faculty than men in comparable jobs.

Another prohibited form of sex discrimination is sexual harassment. Unwelcome sexual advances, requests for sexual favors, and verbal or physical conduct of a sexual nature constitute sexual harassment when:

- the person must submit to such activity in order to be hired
- the person's consent or refusal is used in making an employment decision such as a raise or promotion
- such conduct unreasonably interferes with the person's work performance or creates an intimidating, hostile, or offensive working environment

If you are passed over for a promotion or denied benefits in favor of an employee who has submitted to sexual advances, you are also the victim of sexual harassment. Harassment can occur from anyone, not only your superiors.

> *Sexual harassment was found in one case when female employees were required to wear revealing uniforms and suffer derogatory comments from passersby.*

Claims of sexual harassment may also be made by men.

> *A jury awarded $196,500 in damages to a man who claimed his supervisor demoted him when he refused her sexual advances. According to court testimony, the employee and his supervisor met one night in a hotel room, but the employee refused to continue the relationship. The man proved that as a result of his refusal he was demoted and passed over for a promotion.*

In order to prove sexual harassment, you must document your claim. If you are being teased on the job, complain in writing to a supervisor (see Figure 1.3). Judges, arbitrators, and Equal Employment Opportunity special investigators are more willing to award or recommend damages when a formal complaint was made yet the harassment continued.

Discuss the incident(s) with coworkers to discover if any of them have been victims of similar abuse. One of the elements of proof required in a sexual harassment case is that the employer knew or should have known of the offensive conduct and failed to take corrective action.

Race discrimination. Federal and state laws protect minority workers from discrimination. You cannot be denied a job, fired, or denied a transfer or promotion on the basis of race. Prerequisites for employment that have a discriminatory impact (asking a minority applicant at the hiring interview if he or she has an arrest record or poor credit background) are illegal. If you believe you have been denied an employment opportunity on the basis of race, contact your local EEOC office for assistance.

Handicap discrimination. Most states prohibit discrimination on the basis of physical handicaps. In addition, Congress passed the Americans with Disabilities Act in 1990 to strengthen the rights of handicapped workers. It is now illegal to deny employment to a handicapped person who is capable of performing the job in question, and decisions not to hire an applicant because of a physical or medical condition are closely scrutinized. The Rehabilitation Act of 1973, enforced by the U.S. Department of Labor, prohibits job applicants from being denied employment merely because they have a history of physical or mental impairment that has been cured. In addition, federal law requires employers who receive federal aid to recruit, hire, and promote qualified handicapped persons. It is also illegal for an employer to claim that hiring a person with disabilities would increase insurance costs.

Finally, companies with more than 25 employees (15 after July 1994) are required to make existing facilities used by employees readily accessible to and usable by individuals with disabilities and provide disabled workers with more liberal part-time or modified work schedules or reassignment to an easier vacant position. Other accommodations such as ramps and special eating facilities for people with wheelchairs must also be provided.

Religious discrimination. The EEOC has created guidelines with respect to religious discrimination. Employers have an obligation to make reasonable accommodations to the religious needs of employees and prospective employees. An employer must give you time off for the Sabbath or holy day observance, except in an emergency. In such an event, the employer may give leave without pay, may require you to make up equivalent time, or may allow you to charge the time against any other leave with pay except sick pay. However, these protections may not apply to employees in certain health and safety occupations or to an employee whose presence is essential on a given day. It also does not apply to private employers who can prove that an employee's absence would cause severe business hardship.

Enforcing Your Rights

Recognizing discrimination is only part of the battle; you must take proper steps to enforce your rights. The law entitles victims of discrimination to recover a variety of damages. This includes

- reinstatement
- job hiring
- wage adjustments, back pay, and double back pay

- promotions
- recovering legal fees, expert witness fees, filing costs, damages for emotional pain and suffering, and punitive damages up to $300,000
- instituting an affirmative action program on behalf of fellow employees
- obtaining a jury trial

Your most important step is to file a formal complaint with the EEOC or other appropriate agency to begin the process. No one can stop you from filing a complaint; the law forbids employers from threatening reprisals or retaliation (such as loss of a promotion) when action is taken.

The following facts must be included in the complaint:

- your name
- the names, business address, and business telephone numbers of all persons who committed and/or participated in the discriminatory act(s)
- specific events, dates, and facts to support why the act(s) were discriminatory (statistics, whether other employees or individuals were discriminated against, and, if so, the person or persons victimized, and by whom)

It is not necessary for the complaint to be lengthy or elaborate. The purpose is to allege sufficient facts to trigger an investigation. The advantage of filing a complaint with the EEOC is that charges of discrimination are initiated and investigated at no cost to you. If the complaint seems plausible, the EEOC will develop the claim on your behalf.

Once a formal complaint is received, the EEOC assigns it a number. A copy of the complaint, together with a request for a written response, is sent to the employer, who must respond to the charges within several weeks. After charges and countercharges have been examined by an EEOC investigator, the employer is invited to attend a no-fault conference to negotiate an informal settlement. Approximately 40 percent of all complaints are disposed of this way. The conference is conducted by an experienced EEOC representative. Considerable pressure is placed on the employer to offer a money settlement or some other form of restitution because the EEOC will conduct a formal investigation if a settlement is not reached, and an employer's business records, employment applications, interoffice memos, and pay records may be examined in detail by investigators.

If your case cannot be settled at the conference, several options are available: the EEOC may refer the matter to an appropriate state or local human rights agency for action; the EEOC or Department of Justice may commence a lawsuit for you and/or others similarly situated (a class action lawsuit); or you can hire a lawyer and sue the employer privately.

The advantage of suing an employer privately is that you may reach a settlement faster. However, private lawsuits can be expensive.

There is one loophole in the law. Small employers (those with 15 or fewer employees) may be exempt from sanctions under federal laws. In such an event it may be possible to sue the company for discrimination under pertinent state law, so research your state's law where applicable.

Health and Safety

The 1970 Occupational Safety and Health Act requires every employer to provide a safe and healthful workplace. The Occupational Safety and Health Administration (OSHA) issues regulations on worker safety that employers must follow. OSHA inspectors visit work sites to ensure that employers adhere to the rules. Penalties are sometimes imposed (fines up to $10,000 for each violation and/or imprisonment up to six months) for employers who willfully or repeatedly violate OSHA laws or fail to correct hazards within fixed time limits.

The Occupational Safety and Health Act requires every employer to provide a safe and healthful workplace.

The Occupational Safety and Health Act allows workers to:

- refuse to perform work in a dangerous environment—for example, in the presence of toxic substances, fumes, or radioactive materials
- strike to protest unsafe conditions
- initiate an OSHA inspection of dangerous working conditions by filing a safety complaint
- participate in OSHA inspections and prehearing conferences, and review inspection hearings
- assist the OSHA compliance officer in determining that violations have been corrected

One of the most important aspects of the law is that employers cannot fire, demote, or transfer workers who assert their health and safety rights to a union, OSHA, or any other federal, state, or local agency empowered to investigate or regulate such conditions.

> *In one recent case, seven machine-shop workers walked off their jobs, claiming it was too cold to work. The company fired them, stating they violated company rules by stopping work without notifying the foreman. The workers filed a complaint alleging that this was an unfair labor practice. The U.S. Supreme Court ruled that the employees had a constitutional right to strike over health and safety conditions, and that the firing violated the law. The workers were awarded back pay and job reinstatement as a result.*

Generally, you should not refuse to engage in work that you consider dangerous or unhealthy unless it would place you in imminent danger of serious injury or death. Rather than walking off the job, complain about potentially dangerous or unhealthy conditions to your union, employer, or OSHA.

If you believe you have been punished for exercising your safety and health rights, contact the nearest OSHA area office within 30 days of the time you discover you have been punished. A union representative or attorney-in-fact can file the complaint if you are unable to do so. You must tell an OSHA officer what happened and who was involved; OSHA then investigates. OSHA will ask your employer to restore your job, earnings, and benefits if you have been illegally punished. If necessary, an OSHA representative can go to federal court to protect your rights.

On-the-Job Injuries and Workers' Compensation

Recent developments in workers' compensation cases have enabled some employees to sue their employers directly for their injuries. Workers may benefit substantially if this trend continues because, under traditional workers' compensation, employees are entitled to a predetermined amount of compensation for injuries and nothing more. Critics of the system claim that money paid to injured workers is less than the average jury verdict for similar injuries outside the workplace.

New legal theories are being asserted to circumvent workers' compensation. For example, in one recent case, an employee working for a scaffold manufacturer was injured by a defective scaffold. The worker sued the company directly for his injuries. His lawyer asserted that the company was accountable as a manufacturer, not as an employer. The court agreed.

Some states are allowing employers to be sued for intentionally causing worker injuries. One employee proved that she contracted asbestosis on the job. She claimed the company was liable because it fraudulently concealed the origins of her disease; she was able to recover damages directly from the company for her injuries.

Workers' compensation may not preclude you from recovering additional damages. Contact a lawyer immediately if you are injured while working.

Smoke-Free Environment

The right to work in a smoke-free environment is being upheld with increasing regularity through the passage of state laws, city ordinances, federal legislation, and case decisions. Various federal agencies, including the Merit Board and the EEOC, have ruled that employers must take reasonable steps to keep smoke away from workers.

The following strategies may help you if you desire to work in a smoke-free environment:

1. Gather the facts. Document the environment and conditions of your work location to support your request. Determine the number of smokers, type of ventilation, physical arrangement of desks, and how often people smoke.
2. Acquire medical proof. Visit a doctor if you suffer an illness from working in a smoke-filled environment. Note the prescriptions

and amount of time lost from work. It is also a good idea to visit your employer's doctor to document your condition.

3. Speak to management. Present management with a letter from your doctor stating your need to work in a smoke-free area. If possible, request the transfer collectively with other workers.
4. Confirm your grievance in writing. After the initial discussion, document your request by presenting management with a letter (see Figures 1.4A and 1.4B).
5. Speak to a lawyer. If you receive a negative response or no response from your employer, consult a lawyer, who can assert several options on your behalf. For example, he or she can assist you in presenting demands directly to the employer or union representative, file an action in court, contact OSHA, or sue the employer under the Equal Employment Opportunity Act. Legal fees are sometimes paid to successful litigants under these acts.

   Although such action is probably illegal, your employer may fire or penalize you for enforcing your rights. Consider this possibility before you decide to retain a lawyer.
6. Contact an appropriate agency for further information. Your regional Department of Labor, Department of Health, or OSHA office will provide you with more information. In addition, you may wish to contact the Group Against Smoking Pollution (GASP) at 105 Mountain Avenue, Summit, N.J., (908) 273-9368. GASP maintains a list of pertinent cases, regulations, and lawyers who are knowledgeable in this area.
7. Speak to a doctor about workers' compensation. If you incur medical expenses due to smoke-related on-the-job illness, discuss filing a workers' compensation claim with your doctor.

Protecting Valuable Ideas

Other issues that might cost you money in the workplace have to do with your own special talents—particularly a marketable idea or device that you have developed.

The law generally states that ideas belong to no one and are there for the taking. An idea is presumed to be a work made for hire and property of the employer if an employee offers it voluntarily without contracting to receive additional compensation.

However, don't give away your ideas. The following strategies will protect your rights:

1. Crystallize your ideas, method, or process in writing. This is essential to prove you are the creator of a valuable idea.
2. Be sure the writing is detailed and specific. This can increase your chances of proving the idea is a protectable property interest. For example, if you write a proposal for a unique and original television show, fully describe the characters, budget, and script dialogue rather than briefly discuss the concept of the show.
3. Avoid volunteering ideas. In one famous case, a homemaker mailed an unsolicited cheesecake recipe to a baking company. The recipe was used and became a popular money-maker. When the woman sued the company for damages, the court ruled that no recovery was obtainable because the homemaker voluntarily gave her idea to the company.
4. Negotiate a method of compensation. Always acknowledge your compensation arrangement in writing (see Figure 1.5).
5. Get a receipt. If you cannot obtain an acknowledgment, get a receipt stating that you submitted an idea, that the idea was offered in confidence, that you will be paid if the idea is used, and that the idea cannot be used without your consent.
6. Avoid signing releases. Some companies and individuals ask creators to sign releases stating they assume no obligation in reading the material. Don't sign such a release. However, if you do sign one, you may be able to protect yourself. Wait a few days, then send a letter to the organization, reminding them you are the creator of the idea that you submitted. This may help protect you in the event the idea is used without your consent.
7. Make copies. Keep copies of all materials and letters that you send to others. For proof that they are sent and received, send materials by certified mail, return receipt requested.
8. Speak to a lawyer. It is best to consult a lawyer whenever you want to protect a valuable idea. This is especially important if you develop an idea that can be patented.

STEPS TO TAKE
WHILE WORKING FOR YOUR EMPLOYER

- *Save all correspondence, copies of records, and other documents.*
- *Notify your employer immediately if you discover errors in your salary, bonus, or commissions.*
- *Do not accept reductions in your salary or other benefits, particularly if you have a written contract that prohibits oral modifications of important terms.*
- *Recognize your rights to privacy, to unionize, and to health and safety in the workplace, and seek competent legal counsel at once if your rights are violated.*

WHAT TO DO IF YOU ARE FIRED

The postemployment phase is just as important as knowing how to be hired properly and enforcing your on-the-job rights. Many workers are fired unfairly, and millions of dollars in post-termination benefits are forfeited each year by people who fail to recognize what they are legally entitled to.

Unfair Discharge

Many state and federal laws protect workers from unfair discharge. Dismissals based on the following are illegal, and you can receive money damages by proving you were fired primarily for any of these reasons. This is true even if you were hired at will without a written contract.

- age
- sex
- race, national origin, or religion
- union membership or participation in a union or political activity
- group activity to protest unsafe work conditions

- refusal to commit an unlawful act on the employer's behalf (commit perjury or fix prices)
- reporting alleged violations of the law (whistle-blowing)
- performing a public obligation such as attending jury duty
- being sued for nonpayment of a debt or wage garnishment
- exercising statutory rights or privileges (filing a workers' compensation claim)

Four common causes of unfair firings deserve special mention:

Whistle-blowing. The law protects workers who reveal abuses of authority. Some states have a Whistle-blower's Protection Act that protects employees from retaliation after they report suspected violations of laws or regulations. These statutes provide specific remedies, including reinstatement with back pay, restoration of seniority and lost fringe benefits, litigation costs, attorney fees, and a $500 fine. To find out if your state has a similar law, speak to an experienced labor lawyer, legal referral service, or the Civil Liberties Union in your area.

People who work for federal agencies are also protected from reprisals for whistle-blowing.

> *A nurse was dismissed after reporting abuses of patients at a Veterans Administration medical center. She sought reinstatement and damages before a federal review panel and was reinstated and awarded $7,500 in back pay.*

Firing to deny accrued benefits. The law obligates employers to deal in good faith with longtime employees. Workers sometimes receive money damages when they prove this covenant has been violated.

If you are fired just before you are supposed to receive anticipated benefits (an earned bonus, accrued pension, profit sharing, or commissions due) and have reason to suspect you were fired to be denied these benefits, consult a lawyer immediately. (However, if an employer fires you for a lawful reason—that is, for cause—the fact that you are about to become eligible for a substantial benefit may not make the firing illegal.)

Absence from work. You can be fired for absence from work due to illness unless your union or written employment contract prohibits this.

> *A man with 40 years of service claimed he was fired so his company could avoid paying commissions otherwise due him on a $5 million sale. A court found this to be true and awarded him substantial money even though he had been hired at will.*

> *A woman was fired after working 13 years without a written contract. The court ruled that the company did this to deprive her of the vesting of pension benefits in her fifteenth year of service. The employee was awarded $75,000 in damages.*

But you cannot be fired for asserting a workers' compensation claim. If you are penalized after making such a claim, contact your local workers' compensation board to file a formal complaint.

Maternity leave. Numerous federal and state laws prohibit employers from firing or demoting workers on the basis of pregnancy. Many states provide disability benefits and sick leave to pregnant women; in other states, an extended unpaid maternity leave or child-care leave can be granted only at the discretion of the employer. If the employer permits extended child-care leave, EEOC guidelines require male employees to receive the same benefits. In most states, however, you generally do *not* have the right to get your job back when you seek to return to work after giving birth.

So, if you work without a written contract of a fixed duration, are not a tenured public employee or civil servant, and do not belong to a union, your employer is generally free to fire you for any reason at all, provided the reason does not involve discrimination or is based on a protected form of conduct such as attending jury duty, filing a workers' compensation claim, being absent for a few hours to vote, and so on.

However, some employers have written progressive disciplinary programs for employees that may have to be followed before a firing. Even though they are not unionized, some companies also have written grievance procedures that would enable a fired employee to formally protest the action.

What to Do When You Are Fired

Most employers fire workers without warning. However, the fact that you are axed suddenly does not mean you should accept fewer benefits than you are entitled to. The following strategies can help increase severance benefits and/or damages in the event you are fired:

1. Stall for time. Do not panic or scream at your boss when informed of the bad news. Request extra time to think things over. This may allow you to learn important facts and negotiate a better settlement. *If possible, avoid accepting the company's first offer.*
2. Review your employment contract or letter of agreement. If you signed a contract, reread it. Review what it says about termination. For example, can you be fired at any time without cause, or must the employer send you written notice before the effective termination date? It is essential to know what the contract says in order to map out an effective action plan.
3. Ascertain why you are being fired. This can help in the event you decide to sue your former employer. For example, once you receive reasons for being fired, the employer may be precluded from offering additional reasons at a trial or arbitration. Thus, it is a good idea to request a written explanation of why you were discharged.

    You may have grounds to initiate a lawsuit if an employer refuses to tell you why you were fired. Some states, including Missouri, have *service letter statutes*—laws that require companies to specify in *writing* the reasons for an employee's termination.
4. Learn who made the decision to fire you. You may discover you were fired for petty reasons (such as jealousy) and can be reinstated. Usually, however, there is little you can do other than negotiate a better severance deal.
5. Ask to see your personnel file. Some states permit terminated workers to review and copy the contents of their personnel files. Sometimes these files do not support firing decisions because they contain favorable recommendations and comments. If you can be

fired only for cause and the company gives you specific reasons why you were fired, your file may demonstrate that such reasons are factually incorrect and/or legally insufficient. If this occurs, you may have a strong case against the former employer for breach of contract.

Even if you fail to discover pertinent information, the contents of your file will help you be better prepared for future interviews. Make copies of all recommendations and letters of praise. In addition, add your own explanations and supporting documentation to the file if you discover inaccurate comments.

6. Reconstruct promises. If promises were made by upper management, recall the time and place, and whether these statements were made in the presence of witnesses. The facts surrounding your employment history may justify a finding that you were fired improperly. For example, if the company president told you at the hiring interview "Don't worry, we never fire anyone except for cause," this may be sufficient to create rights in the event you are fired. Some courts are ruling that oral promises of job security are binding even though employment is not for a definite term.

7. Review employment manuals. Language in company policy manuals is sometimes viewed as promises employees may rely on. Some courts have ruled that provisions in personnel manuals and handbooks distributed to employees are enforceable against employers.

Look for answers to the following questions:

- Who is authorized to fire you?
- Must the firing decision be approved by a committee?
- Must you be given written reasons for the firing?
- Can you obtain a copy of your personnel file?
- Must formal procedures be followed (do you have the right to argue before a grievance committee)?
- Must you be given a final warning before the firing is effective?
- Must you first be asked if you are willing to take a job demotion?
- Are there set rules regarding severance benefits?
- Must you be fired only for cause?

Handbooks and manuals can be used as bargaining tools to effectuate a better settlement. If the employer fails to act in a manner specified in its manual, it may be violating an important contractual obligation.

1. Did you sign an employment application? Employment applications sometimes contain important employment terms. Review this document; you may discover that you were fired improperly.
2. Avoid signing exit agreements. Exit agreements, releases, and covenants not to sue can deprive you of valuable rights. Never sign one without the advice of a lawyer.
3. Request a negotiating session. Lower-level employees often have difficulty arranging a negotiating session. However, many executives are granted time to consider a company's first offer and negotiate a better deal.

Post-Termination Benefits

It is unlikely you will get your job back once the firing decision has been made. Your main concern is to receive clarification on accrued wages and available wage equivalents. Discuss the following points with your former employer:

Wages. According to personnel experts, the rule of thumb for severance pay is one month's pay for each year on the job, but this varies by industry and company. However, consider these strategies: Try to stay on the payroll as long as possible; ask for severance pay in one lump sum rather than in installments; discuss relocation allowances, vacation pay, overtime, and unused sick pay. Request additional payments as compensation for allowing the employer to fire you without notice.

Bonus. How will your bonus be computed? If you were entitled to receive a bonus at the end of a full year, ask for it now, arguing that the termination deprived you of the right to receive the bonus. If that doesn't work, insist that your bonus be prorated to the amount of time you worked during the year.

Pension and profit-sharing benefits. The law requires employers to furnish employees with *precise* details regarding the nature and amount of their pension and profit-sharing benefits when they resign or are fired.

Employers are obligated to pay "vested" pension and profit-sharing benefits even if an individual decides to sue his former employer. To learn the vesting rules of your plan, consult your personnel office or union representative. Look into pension and 401(k) rules to determine whether you can move your money to other financial instruments without penalty.

Medical coverage. Does medical coverage stop the day you are fired, or is there a grace period (typically 30 days)? Ask for a copy of the policy. Do you have the option of extending coverage beyond the grace period? If so, what is your contribution to the premium charge? Does it cover your spouse and family? If no medical coverage extension is offered, speak to the company's group insurer representative. You may be able to obtain a reasonable medical *conversion policy*. If you are married and your spouse is working, check to see if you are or can be covered under your spouse's health policy. It may not be necessary to purchase additional coverage.

The federal Consolidated Omnibus Budget Reconciliation Act (COBRA) was enacted in 1986. The most important provisions of this law require some private employers (those who employ more than 20 workers on a typical business day) to continue to make group health insurance available to workers who are discharged from employment. Most people benefit, since the cost of maintaining such insurance is cheaper. The individual pays for coverage at the employer's group rate rather than the cost of an individual policy.

All employees who are discharged as a result of a voluntary or involuntary termination (with the exception of those who are fired for gross misconduct) may elect to continue plan benefits currently in effect at their own cost provided the employee or beneficiary makes an initial payment within 30 days of notification and is not covered under Medicare or any other group health plan. The law also applies to qualified beneficiaries who were covered by the employer's group health plan the day before the discharge. Thus, for example, if the employee chooses not to continue such coverage, his or her spouse or dependent children may elect continued coverage at their own expense. The extended coverage period is 18 months upon the termination of the covered employee; upon the death, divorce, or legal separation of the covered employee, the benefit coverage is 36 months to spouses and dependents.

Life insurance. Inquire about life insurance coverage and ask for a copy of the policy. Some group life insurance plans permit terminated employees to convert the policy to other life insurance within a specific time period. Be sure you know the manner and time period required to exercise the conversion privilege.

Your cover story. Clarify how the news of your departure will be announced. Discuss the story to be told to outsiders—for example, that you resigned for "personal reasons" or the department was down-sizing. Will your employer furnish you with favorable references when you look for a new job? Some employees discover that a former employer is making inaccurate references that inhibit their chances of obtaining new employment. Take affirmative action if this happens to you. For example, send a certified letter to your former employer to protect your rights (see Figure 1.6). This may establish grounds for a defamation lawsuit if the employer continues to make inaccurate statements.

Don't be forced into retirement or resignation based on age because of the demanding nature of the job (such as fire fighter). Think twice if you are offered the opportunity to resign rather than being fired. Although it sounds better, by accepting the offer you may be relinquishing valuable benefits, including unemployment compensation, contributory savings, and other accrued benefits. For example, when you resign from a job, you may be entitled to receive money personally contributed to a pension plan, but you generally *lose* any funds contributed by your employer except to the extent those contributions may have become "vested." Analyze your benefits package carefully before making such a decision.

Other perks. Some employees receive office space, telephone, secretarial help, and the continued use of a company car while looking for employment. Your employer might even agree to tide you over with a loan.

Outplacement guidance. Many employers provide résumé assistance, secretarial help, and job-search expense money to dismissed workers. Others provide outplacement guidance and career counseling.

Additional Points to Remember When You Are Fired

Confirm your agreement in writing. After you have reached a severance agreement with your employer, send a certified letter, return receipt requested, to protect your rights. The letter may serve to clarify points that are still ambiguous as well as document the deal that has been made. In addition, if the employer fails to abide by an important term, such a letter may increase your chances of success if you decide to sue for breach of contract.

Apply for unemployment benefits. Unemployment benefits will help tide you over until you obtain another job. However, you may be denied benefits if you voluntarily left your job, were fired for misconduct, or refused a valid job offer. You can ask for a hearing if you feel benefits were unfairly denied.

Look for work. If you are fired illegally but do not make a good-faith effort to obtain employment, a court may reduce damages by the amount you could have earned in your new job. This is called "mitigation of damages." Many employees who are wrongfully terminated think they can sit back while suing their former employers. This is not true. The law requires you to accept a job with a comparable rate of salary and duties if one is offered.

However, you are not required to relocate or accept a job in a different line of work. If you do not secure employment but make reasonable efforts to obtain a similar job, you will be entitled to all damages under the terms of your contract.

How to Resign Properly

A mistake can expose you to a lawsuit and cause you to forfeit valuable benefits. Careful planning may provide a smooth transition without legal repercussion. Review the following strategies whenever you consider resigning from a job.

Plan ahead. If you believe you will soon be fired, look for a replacement job before the ax falls. People with jobs have better negotiating strength than people out of work. It is legal to spend time soliciting and negotiating a new job provided you do not actually start working (i.e., calling on customers) while employed at your current position.

Sign a written contract with your new employer. This is essential. Never resign from a job until you sign a written employment contract with your new employer. This protects you if the new employer changes his or her mind and decides not to hire you, or tries to fire you after a short period of time.

Review your prior contract or letter of agreement. Learn what it says regarding termination and be sure to comply with those terms. For example, if the contract states that you can resign provided written notice is sent certified mail 60 days prior to the effective termination date, you must send timely notice before you resign. Failure to do so could result in the employer suing you for breach of contract.

Offer notice. It is best to offer notice even if it isn't required. This courtesy gives the employer time to seek a replacement. It also gives you additional time to negotiate a satisfactory settlement before you walk out the door. Two weeks' notice is satisfactory in most situations.

Should you resign by letter? Contrary to popular belief, it is not necessary to resign by letter. In fact, it may be advantageous not to do so. However, if you want to clarify your resignation benefits or put yourself on record that your resignation will not take effect for several weeks, confirm this in writing. Keep the letter brief and avoid giving specific reasons for the resignation, which can preclude you from offering other reasons or tipping your hand in the event of a lawsuit.

Review your benefits package. Be sure you know what you are entitled to.

Keep quiet. Announce the move to friends and business associates only *after* you've told your employer, never before.

Avoid bad-mouthing. Keep the details of the resignation to yourself, especially if the parting is less than amicable. Workers who bad-mouth former employers sometimes wind up being sued for business slander and product disparagement. Other companies withhold severance benefits as a way of getting even. Keep your lips sealed.

Return company property immediately. Return automobile keys, samples, promotional materials, confidential lists, and so on to avoid claims of misappropriation, fraud, and breach of contract. When returning items by mail, be sure to get a receipt to prove delivery. If the company owes you money, you may consider holding the company's property to force a settlement. However, speak to a lawyer before taking such action. Some states permit employees to retain company property as a lien, others do not.

Should you sign a release? A release extinguishes an employee's potential claims. Many companies ask employees to sign releases when they resign. Consider asking for a written release if your contract contains a restrictive covenant or other unfavorable provisions. On the other hand, never sign a release if you believe the employer has mistreated you or you are being asked to waive potentially large claims, such as your right to sue for violations of age or sex discrimination.

Enforce your rights. Speak to a lawyer immediately if you cannot receive what you are entitled to. If you are owed a small sum—say, $750—it may be desirable to commence an action in small claims court in the county where the employer resides or does business (see Chapter 7).

The body of employment law has been created to further fairness and justice. It is there to protect you, but it will be of no help unless you participate in your own defense. Before you make a major move, reread the appropriate portions in this section to be sure you understand the law. If your matter is complicated, speak to an attorney whose practice is primarily labor law.

EMPLOYMENT AGENCY, SEARCH FIRM, AND CAREER-COUNSELING ABUSES

In their eagerness to obtain employment, many individuals are exploited by dishonest employment agencies, search firms, and career counselors. Some applicants are charged exorbitant placement fees. Others pay large, nonrefundable fees for job interviews that do not result in jobs. Still others are asked discriminatory questions at the initial interview or are told to register for courses, for which the agency gets a fee, before they are sent out on interviews.

You can protect yourself from unethical and illegal employment practices if you:

Know the differences between employment agencies, search firms, and career counselors. The primary function of employment agencies is to obtain jobs for clients. Search firms and career counselors perform a variety of services, including résumé and letter preparation, teaching successful interviewing techniques, and providing leads for job openings. They do *not* obtain jobs for applicants.

Understand the ramifications of your arrangement. Ask the following questions before you agree to be represented by an employment agency, search firm, or career counselor:

- Is the firm licensed? In some states, employment agencies are licensed and regulated by the Department of Consumer Affairs. To obtain a license, the agency must fill out a detailed application, post a performance bond, maintain accurate records, and avoid

---

A search firm placed an ad in a nationally known newspaper that read:

We Use Our Contacts, Methods, Experience,
Research Facilities, and Equipment to Obtain
Interviews for You in the Unpublished,
Unadvertised Job Marketplace; Positions are
Available for qualified executives, managers, and
professionals in the $20,000 to $60,000 range in
corporations, associations, and foundations.

The ad attracted several hundred individuals, who reportedly paid advance fees ranging from $500 to $8,000. Most of these people never received any placement assistance or contacts.

---

engaging in illegal acts. Career counselors and search firms do not have to be licensed to conduct business.

- What are the precise services the firm or individual will render?
- What is required of the job applicant (prepare a résumé, buy interviewing attire, etc.)?
- When will the firm or individual earn its fee: When you are offered a job by an acceptable firm, when you accept the job, or when you work a minimum amount of time?
- What is the maximum fee charged?
- Who will pay for the fee, you or the employer? When is it payable?
- What happens if you decide not to accept a job that is offered?
- Is a deposit required once a job is accepted? If so, by whom?
- Will you receive a detailed description of each potential employer before you go on an interview, including the name, address, kind of work to be performed, title, amount of wages or compensation, hours, whether the work is temporary or permanent?
- Will the agency investigate whether the potential employer has defaulted in the payment of salaries to others during the past five years?
- What happens to the fee if you resign or are fired within a short period of time?

- Will the agency help you obtain another job if you are terminated?
- Does the agency have the right to represent you on an exclusive basis?
- What happens to the fee if you become disabled and cannot work?

Confirm your arrangement in writing. Reputable firms will confirm your arrangement in writing. Read the agreement carefully and question all ambiguous terms.

Avoid paying money in advance. It is illegal for employment agencies to charge a fee *before* they find you a job. However, career-counseling and search firms are permitted by law to charge a fee up front. Resist this, if possible. Many people pay money to firms but never receive promised services.

It is illegal for employment agencies to charge a fee before they find you a job.

> *A modeling agency placed an impressive ad in a local newspaper saying that it was looking for attractive children. Parents from hundreds of miles away brought their children in hopes of establishing them in a career. The agency agreed to represent the children provided the parents spent several hundred dollars for pictures and promotional materials. Weeks later, a few black-and-white photographs of the children were received, but that was the last time the parents heard from the agency.*

Do not pay money up front; wait until you are satisfied that the firm is working hard on your behalf.

Recognize abuses before they occur. The following is a list of common employment agency acts that are prohibited under many state laws. It is illegal for an employment agency to:

- induce you to terminate your job so the agency can obtain new employment for you
- publish false or misleading ads

- advertise in newspapers without providing the name and address of the agency
- send you to an employer without obtaining a job order from the employer
- make false representations or promises
- require you to subscribe to publications, pay for advertising costs, enroll in special courses, or pay for additional services
- charge a placement fee when the agency represents that it was a fee-paid job
- discriminate on the basis of sex, race, religion, or age
- require you to complete application forms that obtain different information from male and female applicants

Many of these activities are also illegal if committed by search firms and career-counseling services.

Seek immediate assistance if you have been exploited. If you believe you have been exploited, send a letter to the firm to document your protest. The letter should state the reasons for your dissatisfaction and the manner in which you would like the problem resolved (see Figures 1.7 and 1.8). You can also initiate a suit in small claims court.

FIGURE 1.1 Sample Letter to Human Rights Commission

Your Address
Telephone Number
Date

Director of Appropriate Agency
Anywhere, U.S.A.
Re: Formal Protest Against ABC Employer for Illegal Hiring Practices

To Whom It May Concern:

This letter is a formal complaint against ABC Employer, located at (address).

On (date), I was interviewed by (name of employee) for the position of (title). The interview took place at (location). During this interview, I believe I was asked a variety of illegal questions. The following are the specific questions asked: (name them)

Although I answered some of the questions, I chose not to answer others on the basis of irrelevance.

After the interview, I was told by (name) that the company never hired anyone who refused to answer these questions. Although extremely qualified, I was denied the job.

I believe I was the victim of illegal and discriminatory hiring practices. I understand that your agency has the authority to investigate these charges and institute legal proceedings, if appropriate. Therefore, please investigate this matter on my behalf. You can reach me at the above address and telephone number if you require any additional information or assistance.

Thank you for your cooperation in this matter.

Sincerely,
(Signature)

[Send certified mail, return receipt requested.]

FIGURE 1.2A Sample Employee Letter of Agreement

Your Address
Telephone Number
Date

Name of Corporate Officer
Title
ABC Corporation
Anywhere, U.S.A.

Dear (Name):

Per our discussion, it is agreed that I shall be employed by ABC as a computer analyst for an initial term of two years, beginning January 1, 1993. As compensation for services, I will receive a salary of $30,000 per year payable in equal bimonthly installments on the first and fifteenth day of each month during the employment term.

In addition to my base salary, I will receive an annual bonus of $10,000 payable in equal quarterly installments, and the company will promptly reimburse me for all reasonable business expenses on presentation of appropriate vouchers and records. This bonus will be given as compensation for additional services to be rendered. Upon termination of this agreement for any reason, I shall be entitled to receive my bonus and salary for the remaining period of the quarter in which my termination occurs.

If any of the terms in this letter are not correct, please advise me immediately in writing. Otherwise, this letter shall set forth our understanding of this matter.

I look forward to working for ABC.

Sincerely,
(Signature)

[Send certified mail, return receipt requested.]

FIGURE 1.2B Sample Sales Representative Agreement

Your Address
Telephone Number
Date

Name of Corporate Officer
Title
Company Name
Anywhere, U.S.A.

Re: Sales Agreement

Dear (Name):

This letter will confirm the terms of my engagement as an exclusive sales representative for your company.

I agree to represent the company in the states of Florida, Georgia, and South Carolina for a minimum period of one year, beginning on January 1, 1993.

The above-named territory will be covered exclusively by me, with no other sales reps covering this territory. There will be no house accounts in the territory.

I will receive a commission of 10 percent of the gross invoice for all accepted orders in my territory, regardless of whether the orders are sent by me, received by the company through the mail, or taken at the company's place of business without my assistance.

There will be no deductions from my commission for credits or returns. Commission checks together with commission statements will be sent on the tenth day of the month following the month my orders are accepted.

I will be considered an independent contractor and will be responsible for all applicable social security, withholding, and other employment taxes.

This contract will be automatically renewed for successive one-year terms so long as my yearly gross volume of accepted orders exceeds that of the previous year.

If any of the terms of this letter are incorrect, please advise me immediately in writing. Otherwise, this letter shall set forth our understanding of this matter.

I look forward to working with you.

Sincerely,
(Signature)

[Send certified mail, return receipt requested.]

___

FIGURE 1.3 Sample Letter Protesting Sexual Harassment

___

Date

(Name)
Supervisor
QRS Company
Address

Re: Complaint of Sexual Harassment

Dear (Name),

While working for the company, I have been the victim of a series of offensive acts that I believe constitute sexual harassment.

On (date), I (describe what occurred and with whom). I immediately (describe your reaction) and felt that such conduct should stop. However, on (date), another incident occurred when (describe what occurred and with whom).

I find such behavior intimidating and repugnant. In fact, (describe the physical and emotional impact on you), causing me to be less efficient on the job. Unless such conduct ceases immediately, I will contact the Equal Employment Opportunity Commission to enforce my rights. I do not wish to take such a drastic measure. All I want to do is perform my job in a professional environment.

Thank you for your cooperation in this matter.

Sincerely,
(Signature)

[Send certified mail, return receipt requested.]

___

FIGURE 1.4A Sample Letter Demanding a Smoke-Free Work Environment

---

Date

Name and Title
Department
Company Name and Address

Dear (Name):
   This will confirm the conversations we have had regarding the need to provide me (us) with a work environment free of tobacco smoke. Enclosed is information to support the request to eliminate smoking in work areas.
   Also enclosed is a petition signed by employees in our work location. [If this is an individual request and there is no petition, disregard this paragraph.]
   As my (our) ability to work is constantly undermined by the unhealthy, toxic pollutants to which I (we) am (are) chronically exposed, I (we) will appreciate your giving this request priority. May I (we) expect a reply by (date)?

Very truly yours,
(Signature)

FIGURE 1.4B Sample Follow-up Letter Requesting Smoke-Free Environment

---

(Date)

Name and Title
Department
Company Name and Address

Dear (Name):

   As of this date, I (we) have received no reply to my (our) request of (date).

   [If temporary or interim measures were tried but were unsuccessful, identify them here.]

   To protect my (our) health while in your employ, it is vital that the company provide me (us) with a smoke-free work area so as to comply with the common law requirements of this state. I (we) have asked organizations that are expert in the area of occupational health to provide you with additional information on my (our) behalf.

   I (we) will appreciate your immediate response to this urgent matter.

Sincerely,
(Signature)

[Send copies to middle management, president of company, medical director of company, union representative, and personal physician.]

FIGURE 1.5 Sample Acknowledgment of Receipt of Idea

On this day, I have received from (employee's name) an idea concerning _____, which was presented in the form of _____.

The company acknowledges that it has not used the idea in the past. If used, (employee's name) will be compensated according to the following: _____.*

The employer agrees to maintain the confidentiality of the material submitted to us by (employee's name) and agrees not to disclose it, or the ideas on which it is based, to any person, firm, or entity without the employee's consent.

(Date)   (Employer)

By:
(Employee)

*If compensation is difficult to determine at the time the acknowledgment is prepared, it can state that the employee will be compensated in a manner mutually agreed upon by the parties and that the idea will remain the property of the employee until such formula is determined.

FIGURE 1.6 Sample Letter Protesting Unfavorable Job Reference

Your Address
Telephone Number
Date

(Name of Employer)
Anyplace, U.S.A.

Dear (Name):
On (date) I applied for a job with (name of potential employer). At the interview, I was told that your firm had submitted an inaccurate, unfavorable reference about me.

You supposedly said the reason I was fired was that I was an uncooperative and complaining worker.

This is untrue. In fact, my personnel file, which I copied, contains not one derogatory comment about me.

You are hereby requested to cease making inaccurate statements about my job performance. If you do not comply, I will contact my lawyer and take appropriate legal action.

Thank you for your cooperation in this matter.

Sincerely,
(Signature)

cc: Potential employer

[Send certified mail, return receipt requested.]

FIGURE 1.7 Sample Complaint Letter to Job-Search Firm

Your Address
Telephone Number
(Date)

Name of Firm
(Address)

Dear (Name):

On (date) I responded to an advertisement your firm ran in (name of magazine). The ad specifically promised that your firm could find a job for me as a salesperson in the cosmetics industry. The ad stated that a $250 advance was fully refundable in the event I could not obtain a job paying more than $20,000 per year.

Per your request, and after several telephone conversations, I sent you a check for $250. That was four months ago. Since that time I have received one letter from you, dated _____, which states you are reviewing my employment history.

In view of the fact that I have not obtained full-time employment, I hereby demand the return of my $250, per our agreement.

If I do not receive the money within 14 days from the date of this letter, I shall contact the Department of Consumer Affairs, the Better Business Bureau, the frauds division of the attorney general's office, and my lawyer to commence a formal investigation.

Thank you for your cooperation in this matter.

Sincerely,
(Signature)

[Send certified mail, return receipt requested. If the problem is not resolved to your satisfaction, your next step should be to contact your local Department of Consumer Affairs and Better Business Bureau—see Figure 1.8.]

FIGURE 1.8 **Sample Letter to Department of Consumer Affairs and Better Business Bureau**

Your Address
Telephone Number
(Date)

Commissioner
Department of Consumer Affairs

Re: Formal Complaint Against ABC Employment Agency, License #____

Dear Commissioner:

I hereby make a formal complaint against (name of employment agency). I believe that the firm has committed the following illegal acts (state what they are).

The facts on which I base my allegations are as follows: (state the facts).

On (date), I sent the agency a formal demand letter requesting the return of my deposit. This letter was sent by certified mail, and I received no response. I enclose a copy of the letter for your review.

I request that you convene a formal hearing regarding this matter.

Feel free to contact me at the above address if you need any further assistance or information.

Thank you for your cooperation.

Sincerely,
(Signature)

[Send certified mail, return receipt requested.]

---

2 Avoiding Phony Business and Investment Schemes

INVESTMENT FRAUDS

Phony business opportunities and investment frauds are a common form of consumer exploitation, and many people are defrauded by close friends and relatives as well as strangers!

> *A wealthy, aged widow desperately sought advice from an attorney on how to recover a large sum of money—her life savings—that she had invested with a relative who was the accountant for a business deal that collapsed. She was advised that in her particular case there was little that could be done after the fact.*

The following guidelines can protect you no matter what form of investment you are contemplating. Review these rules *before* sinking your money into a business or investment offering.

First Commandment: Never rely on promises from people you don't know.

Second Commandment: Be wary of people who offer deals over the telephone.

Third Commandment: Be suspicious of deals that offer large returns to anonymous investors.

Fourth Commandment: Be skeptical of deals offered in newspaper and magazine ads; most legitimate business opportunities are not marketed this way.

Fifth Commandment: Never be pressured into making a quick decision. If you are told a once-in-a-lifetime deal will pass by unless you act quickly, chances are good that you are being swindled.

Sixth Commandment: Never invest in a deal until you receive written information. Read the literature thoroughly *before* making any decision.

Seventh Commandment: Investigate the identity of the promoters, organizers, general partners, and other individuals involved in the deal. Do they have a successful track record in other ventures? Ask for bank and credit references.

Eighth Commandment: Analyze how your money will be used. Is it secured? In what is it being invested? Are the organizers receiving an unfair share?

Ninth Commandment: Consult a lawyer, accountant, financial adviser, or other professional before investing large sums in a venture.

Tenth Commandment: Contact the Federal Trade Commission (FTC) or the Federal Bureau of Investigation (FBI) if you have doubts. These agencies maintain a list of companies and individuals who have been indicted and convicted for investment fraud.

FRANCHISE ABUSES

It is estimated that nearly one-third of all U.S. retail sales, amounting to hundreds of billions of dollars in products and services, are conducted from more than 500,000 franchise locations. Millions of people are employed in franchise operations, and tens of thousands of additional franchises start up each year.

The popularity of franchising is due to its unique method of conducting business. For an agreed-upon price, sometimes as little as $5,000, a franchisor grants the right to market products and operate a franchise in a specific location. The franchisee may acquire use of the name, designs, equipment, start-up assistance, and selling methods. Ownership of the venture may or may not remain with the franchisor; more often it does not. The average investment, including equipment and other costs, can exceed $100,000.

Despite the success of franchises, abuses are prevalent. Unsophisticated investors are exploited because they are unable to evaluate franchise offers properly. Some franchisors exaggerate the potential for profit and provide little help if the franchise is not successful. People launch successful businesses but lose them through recapture tactics by franchisors. Others mortgage their homes and invest their life savings on the basis of exaggerated claims of potential profitability.

There are no federal laws specifically governing the franchising industry.

There are no federal laws specifically governing the franchising industry. This adds to the risk of abuse. Whereas some states have laws protecting potential investors from misrepresentation, false and misleading advertising, and fraudulent franchise schemes, others do not.

Protect Yourself

Beware of misleading ads promising high returns. Franchise operators often place deceptive advertisements to attract investors:

FABULOUS BUSINESS OPPORTUNITY THROUGH OWNERSHIP OF YOUR OWN FRANCHISE

ABC Company, the innovator in mattress and bedding franchises, is offering area franchises to select investors. Fantastic return on investment. Guaranteed $1 million sales in the first year. Experience not required. Our employees will train and assist in the start-up. Call for an appointment.

This ad may be misleading in several respects:

- Investors may be required to pay additional money for equipment, training, and start-up assistance. The ad doesn't say this.

- Financially unsuccessful franchises may be sold to anyone who puts up the cash.
- Exclusive territories may be promised but not allotted, with many competitive franchises offered nearby.
- Guaranteed sales may be a fabrication or based on inaccurate figures.

The first step in analyzing franchise ventures is to examine all sales promotion literature and advertisements. Scrutinize claims telling you what to expect in profits, sales, and earnings.

Investigate the franchise. Before beginning serious negotiations, ask for:

- financial statements, bank references, credit references, and other written materials concerning the franchisor, officers, and key executives
- facts about the negative as well as the positive aspects of the venture
- books and records revealing the sales figures of other franchisees (One of the major reasons franchises fail is that investors receive misleading profit projections; reviewing the actual books and records may protect you in this area.)
- a copy of the franchise-offering statement (The Federal Trade Commission requires that all franchises include a detailed description of the business start-ups and applicable fees.)
- the names of other franchisees (Speak to them about their business. Better still, visit their operations.)

Analyze the Key Points of the Deal

Investors sometimes sign franchise agreements without understanding all the ramifications. Know the answers to the following questions to protect your investment:

- How much down payment is required?
- Is a down payment required before negotiations begin? (Most legitimate franchisors do not ask for a deposit until the contract is signed.)

- What is the *entire* fee for your investment?
- Are royalty, licensing, and advertising allowances included in the fee or are they extra? (These charges are often overlooked and can be substantial. If a royalty is not included in the fee—for example, 10 percent of the annual gross sales—be sure you know whether the business will be able to sustain profitability while paying these fees. You must calculate the effect of these expenses on your business before you decide to invest.)
- Can the franchise be terminated without your consent? If so, under what conditions? (Some franchisees lose their businesses as a result of unfair termination provisions in franchise agreements, such as failure to meet lofty sales quotas.)
- How long can you operate your franchise? (Some investors build successful franchises but are required to give the business back after a specified number of years.)
- Will the franchisor provide assistance such as architectural and location site assistance, job training for managers, and so on? Do you have to pay extra for this?
- Can the franchisor exercise control over your business? To what degree?
- Must you buy equipment from the franchisor in order to begin business? What is the entire fee? Is it fair? Are there exorbitant interest payments?
- Are you prohibited from starting the franchise in the location of your choice?
- Can the franchisor refuse to renew the franchise and/or purchase it back from you? How much money, if any, will you receive? How will it be paid? Is the price fair?
- Can you invest in the franchisor's business? Will you obtain a more favorable price for the franchisor's stock?
- Are you required to purchase products exclusively from the franchisor? Do you anticipate delivery problems?
- Are you obligated to do business with or pay commissions to third parties?
- Are you or members of your immediate family required to work at the franchise site?
- Are you relying on specific promises or guarantees? (Be sure to include these in the agreement. For example, if the franchisor

makes claims about your potential earnings, insist that you receive appropriate figures to prove the accuracy of all claims, statistics about the number of franchises and the amount of failures, and the number of franchises that earn *below* the earning claims.)

Consult a competent adviser. Speak to a lawyer, accountant, or financial adviser before you buy. Representing yourself in the purchase of a franchise enterprise is almost always a mistake. A lawyer should negotiate and review your franchise contract. Franchise agreements are complicated documents that are usually prepared by franchisors and contain unfavorable clauses.

Contact a lawyer of your state's attorney general's office immediately if you believe you have been exploited. A number of states have franchise registration statutes that obligate franchisors to file offering statements before selling franchises. Some states require franchisors to provide franchise-offering documents to potential investors *before* a franchise contract can be signed. These laws disallow the sale in the event that the franchise-offering documents are not distributed. In addition, the FTC requires that a franchisor provide a prospective franchisee with an offering circular no later than the first serious meeting or 10 days prior to the execution of the contract. You can also seek remedies under antitrust and common law actions in fraud, misrepresentation, and breach of warranty. The FTC may be able to get you out of the deal if the franchisor has not met its legal obligations.

REAL ESTATE RIP-OFFS

Vast acreage of unimproved land is being subdivided and offered for sale as homesites and retirement spots. You have probably seen slick advertisements proclaiming the advantages of accessible leisure communities and urging people to purchase "a place in the sun." These come-ons are often misleading. The out-of-state purchaser is unfamiliar with the topography, and parcels are frequently overpriced. Despite such ads, it is often untrue that water is available, or that the land is furnished with adequate sewage disposal, road maintenance, electricity, gas, and accessible transportation. In many cases, developers abandon projects before completing elaborate facilities.

Question the accuracy of all promotional claims and advertising literature. The following advertisement is typical.

SUNFLOWER RANCHES IN BOOMING NEVADA
6 ACRES
$2,895 Full Price—No Interest (Price Increases to $3,495 on Oct. 1)
Only $50 down and $20 a month
Near Reno—Fun City of the Southwest

Fly out to our headquarters and view the property.
Lodging and meals at our expense.

LOOK AT THE FOLLOWING FACTS:
1. Nevada's free land is being bought up at an alarming rate.
2. Land values in Nevada are rising rapidly.
3. During the last ten years, Nevada's population increased by 240 percent.
4. The climate is spectacular—no smog or snow, only sun.
5. Each ranch is located near major highways; electricity and water are also provided.
6. The developer is about to complete a fabulous 18-hole golf course and clubhouse.
7. Title guaranteed by warranty deed and title insurance.

Although some states require developers to submit advertisements for approval before they can be released to the public, promoters still manage to disseminate false and misleading advertising.

Scrutinize all claims before speaking to a developer or the sales staff. Unscrupulous developers use a variety of tactics to induce you to buy. One is the "rush game"—"the price will go up tremendously on October 1, so buy now." Another is the "free inducement offer"—if you travel to their development site, they will pay your lodging expenses while you are there. Customers who travel to the site are often manipulated by fast-talking salespeople. Some promoters renege on their promise to pay for lodging; others house prospective buyers in inadequate facilities.

Ask for written documentation to support advertising and promotional claims. One of the best ways to determine if you are dealing with a legitimate land developer is to request copies of documents that are required to be filed by law. Review these documents before you travel to the development site or sign the contract.

The following documents must be filed with appropriate agencies under many state and federal laws:

- purchase agreement embodied in the sales program
- county engineer's report that describes the physical characteristics of the land proposed for development
- title insurance policy
- certificate of registration
- deed and opinion of title
- reports by licensed engineers regarding drainage, accessibility to roads, and availability of drinkable water
- schedule and timetable of all improvements to be performed by the developer
- report from the county stating that the streets and other public places in the subdivided plot will be maintained
- proposed offering statement

According to the federal Interstate Land Sales Full Disclosure Act, developers must file a Statement of Record and Property Report with the Secretary of Housing and Urban Development (HUD) in Washington before large subdivided plots can be sold to the public. In order to be approved by HUD, all statements contained in these documents must be substantiated by supporting affidavits and exhibits. Once approval is obtained, a copy of the property report must be given to each prospective purchaser. If you are not given a copy of the property report before signing the contract, the law allows you to rescind the transaction or sue for damages.

Investigate the developer. Inquire into the financial resources and reputation of the developer. Start out by asking what associations, if any, the developer belongs to. Contact these organizations to learn about the qualifications for membership and how long the developer has been a member. Call the attorney general's office in the state where the land is located to find out if the developer has ever been charged with land fraud or other illegal practices.

When you meet with the developer or his or her representative, ask the following questions before beginning serious negotiations:

- Has a performance bond or other security been posted to assure the completion of facilities or improvements? With whom? Request a copy.
- Who is the lawful owner of the land? If title is held by a corporation or limited partnership, who are the partners? Are there any judgments, liens, or encumbrances against the owner of record?
- What is the track record of the developer? Has he or she completed other developments? (Investigate them.)
- Who are the authorized sales agents? Where are they located? How long have they been in business? Have they worked with the developer on past projects?

Investigate the land. Once you are satisfied with the developer's reputation, familiarize yourself with the physical characteristics and other features of the land. For example, you should know the amount of yearly property taxes and whether there are any hidden costs. The following are important points to consider:

- What is the total purchase price?
- How much money is required as a deposit? Is it refundable?
- What is the down payment?
- What kind of deed and other assurances are you receiving from the seller?
- What are the monthly payments and financing charges?
- Is time of the essence? If the land is supposed to be built on or developed within a certain amount of time, this should be specified in writing.
- Has the land been zoned for special use?
- If the property to be acquired is income producing, do existing leases comply with all federal and state regulations?
- Have special assessments been imposed for local improvements?
- Does the seller have legal authority (power of attorney) to sign the contract if he or she is not the real owner?

- Have you as the buyer received a detailed description of the premises? Have you reviewed it to be sure it is accurate?
- What is the range of selling prices within the development?
- Does the community offer potential for future growth?
- Are there provisions for water, drainage, electricity, gas, telephone lines, and sewage disposal?
- Is there access to main roads?
- Are there recreational and common facilities?
- Are there municipal services such as fire and police protection, medical and dental facilities, public transportation, schools, and shopping?
- Are the premises sold subject to an existing mortgage or can you obtain your own mortgage?

Consult a lawyer to review all documents and represent you at the closing. If you are satisfied with the developer's reputation and the land you are about to purchase, discuss the deal with a lawyer. This is essential in any large real estate transaction.

Avoiding Problems with Real Estate Brokers

An increasing number of complaints are being recorded regarding illegal practices of brokers, agents, and salespeople. Some realtors are engaging in misrepresentation. For example, prospective buyers visit houses and learn that advertised bedrooms are only walk-in closets, or that a den is really a small foyer. Others are victims of discrimination. The following strategies may reduce your chances of being exploited.

Avoid signing binder agreements. Binders set forth key terms of the proposed sale, and they have legal consequences: They obligate sellers to pay realtor commissions when the broker produces a willing, able, and ready purchaser, even if the deal fails to go through. Many sellers of homes and other real estate have been held liable for the broker's commission after the transaction has fallen through.

If an agent insists that you sign a binder, you may wish to insert language similar to the following for your protection:

The full brokerage commission to be earned shall be $XXX. However, said commission is not to be considered earned until the full

> *A couple was sued for $8,000, which represented the broker's commission on a deal that was never consummated. The couple signed the broker's standard binder agreement, which stated that they agreed to sell their home for $120,000. A day after the agreement was signed, the broker located a suitable purchaser. However, the couple notified the broker that day that they had second thoughts about selling and wished to take their home off the market. The couple was sued by the broker and lost the case.*

purchase price is paid to the seller and the deed is delivered to the purchaser. If this is not accomplished for any reason whatsoever, the broker shall have no claim for commission or compensation in connection with this transaction and shall promptly refund all money held on deposit.

This clause may protect you from paying a commission on a sale that is not finalized, and some brokers may agree to it.

Deal only with a reputable broker. About 600,000 of the 2.5 million individuals licensed to sell real estate are members of associations such as the National Association of Realtors (NAR). Local chapters of the NAR police their members and conduct formal hearings on complaints. Realtors who misappropriate money or engage in illegal practices are subject to disciplinary sanctions, including removal from access to multiple-listing services, fines, and suspension from the association. By dealing with a realtor who is a member in good standing of a similar organization, you may avoid problems. (Some states have licensing boards that oversee and police activity. Research the law in your state for more information.)

Interview the broker before hiring him or her. Select an experienced broker with a good reputation. You may be able to negotiate the amount of commission and the length of representation. Many independent brokers will reduce their fees when they don't have to share commissions with other brokers, so don't hesitate to ask for a reduction of the broker's commission before agreeing to representation. Confirm the terms of your arrangement in writing to avoid misunderstandings (see Figure 2.1).

Deal with real estate brokers rather than salespeople if possible. In order to qualify as a broker, an individual must have a certain amount of classroom instruction and actual selling experience, and must pass a state exam. Salespeople usually must pass a less rigorous exam and are restricted to working under a broker's supervision. Thus, real estate brokers are typically more knowledgeable than salespeople. Nevertheless, an accountant or attorney specializing in real estate law may provide the best information about which mortgage is right for you.

Understand that realtors often promote their exclusive listings that maximize sales commissions even if such listings are not in your best interest. In an open listing, all the agents in an area have access to the property and the commission goes to the agency that produces the buyer. In some cases, the original listing agency splits the commission with the agency that produces the buyer. In an exclusive listing, one agency is the sole marketer of the property for an agreed-upon period of time. If you are the seller, consider a multiple listing service immediately. Offering an agency an exclusive can limit prospects and leave you open to some abuses—i.e., the agent could sell to a crony and cheat you. However, it is a good idea to retain the right to show and sell the property yourself (in effect, competing with the agency) and not be obligated to pay a commission to the agency if you bring about the sale.

If you are a buyer. The broker represents the seller. Therefore, the agent may misrepresent the property, pretend there are higher bids to get you to increase yours, or practice racial discrimination by refusing to show you a house in a particular neighborhood or discouraging your interest.

Remember that it is illegal to be denied access to a house or apartment because of mental or physical handicap, national origin, sexual preference, or gender.

Remember that it is illegal to be denied access to a house or rented apartment because of mental or physical handicap, national origin, sexual preference, or gender.

Take immediate action if you have been exploited. If you have a problem with a real estate broker, agent, or salesperson that cannot be resolved, contact the Regional Board of Realtors in your state as well as the local chapter of the National Association of Realtors. These boards may investigate your written complaint and conduct a formal hearing on your behalf (see Figure 2.2).

> *A jury recently awarded $15,350 in punitive and compensatory damages to a private fair-housing group that had commenced a class action lawsuit against a realty firm. The group alleged that the broker refused to show rental apartments owned by a particular landlord to minority applicants. Nonwhite prospective tenants were repeatedly told there were no vacancies or that vacant apartments had been rented. Although private discrimination is sometimes difficult to prove, numerous trained testers (i.e., minority members working for the group who sought to rent apartments in the buildings) testified at the trial. The court is now in the process of determining if the landlords should pay $500,000 in legal fees for the many years of litigation. Moreover, the brokers may lose their real estate licenses and suffer fines and other penalties.*

Tips When Buying a Home

- Remember: The broker works for the seller.
- Do not agree to look at homes or property consistently above your maximum price range or not in your preferred location.
- Be wary if the broker offers you legal or tax advice.
- Do not let the broker argue with you about an offer you wish to make. It is the broker's responsibility to communicate all offers to the seller.
- If you are unhappy with a broker, switch to someone else. If you are assigned a salesperson at the agency and feel that the individual is not qualified or working in your best interest, demand to work with the president of the agency. You are probably under no obligation to stay with one broker at a firm even if that person or the firm has spent much time showing you homes or property.
- It is a good idea to work with a broker who is participating in a multiple listing service. You will have a wider range of properties to choose from.
- Inspect real estate before you purchase or make an offer. Hire an

independent housing inspector or engineer to evaluate plumbing, wiring, heating, roofing, septic system, well, and foundation.

Rentals

There are several areas where renters are often exploited. To guard against common schemes and abuses, make sure of the following:

- The broker, if you use one, works for you, not for the landlord.
- You deal only with a licensed broker.
- If you are the landlord, avoid giving the broker an exclusive right to rent the property; retain the right to rent it yourself or to allow other brokers to assist you. Carefully review any broker's agreement before signing.
- If you are a tenant, pay a broker's fee only after you rent an apartment found by that broker.
- Do not rent an apartment based on a floor plan. Inspect the apartment carefully—flush the toilet, turn on the oven, make sure the windows open, and so on—before you sign the lease.
- Take your time. Do not be pressured to make a snap decision.
- Always read the lease carefully before you sign. If you are leasing property on behalf of a business or company, avoid personal liability. Never personally guarantee payment of the lease if you can help it. For example, if applicable, always sign the lease in your official capacity (e.g., "John Smith, President," not "John Smith").

Other terms to consider include negotiating for the security deposit to be placed in a separate *interest-bearing account* with you getting the interest on a yearly basis and negotiating for the right to lease with an option to buy the property after a certain period of time. This may substantially reduce the final purchase price. Negotiate for painting, upgrade, or replacement of old appliances. Avoid signing leases with clauses:

- eliminating the right to trial by jury
- forcing you to pay large attorney fees when the landlord commences legal proceedings
- giving large increases on top of the base rent (Hidden costs in leases often include tax escalation provisions, construction and alteration

of the premises fees, insurance obligations, utility charges, and many other costs. Be sure you understand the total bill to be incurred before signing on the dotted line.)
- giving the landlord the right to evict you when the rent is not received within *x* days of the beginning of the month (Retain the right to be notified *in writing* before any legal action is commenced so you will be given additional time and the opportunity to cure any alleged violations or breaches of the lease.)

Leases are sometimes such complicated documents that you may want them reviewed carefully by an attorney or accountant before signing. If you use the standard type of form found in a stationery store, review it carefully: Such forms often contain clauses that can cause difficulty later.

HOME IMPROVEMENT AND BUILDING CONTRACTOR ABUSES

Americans spend over a hundred billion dollars a year on building renovation and home improvements. The Better Business Bureau (BBB) says it receives more contractor-related complaints than any other form of complaint. Abuses include salespeople pressuring consumers into signing inadequate contracts that fail to incorporate oral promises and contractors using inferior materials that do not satisfy building code requirements or overcharging for jobs that are never satisfactorily completed. Whether you employ a general contractor or a specialist such as a plumber or carpenter, you can enforce your rights.

Choosing a Contractor

Choosing the right contractor can save you a great deal of grief.

Deal only with a licensed contractor. Most Departments of Consumer Affairs and/or Better Business Bureaus require that contractors be licensed. Some require that contractors post a bond and sign affidavits before issuing licenses. A license does not guarantee reliability or competence, but it is a step in the right direction. Contact the above agencies to discover whether a contractor is licensed. Inquire whether any complaints or lawsuits have recently been lodged against the contractor.

Ask for references from customers and suppliers. Confirm all references.

Get a written estimate. The estimate should include a description of materials to be purchased (color, size, weight, and grade). Try to obtain written estimates from several contractors to make valid comparisons. Some contractors charge for written estimates, so be sure you know how much the estimate will cost *before* asking for it.

Recognize common schemes. You can avoid being exploited by recognizing common illegal practices:

- Farming out work to unqualified subcontractors: Inquire who will actually do the work before you hire the contractor, and include this in the contract.
- Low-price bait ads: Unscrupulous contractors sometimes agree to provide inexpensive work but send an "engineer" to persuade you to accept a more expensive package.
- Rebates, discounts, or gifts: If you are relying on promises of gifts (such as a free television) when accepting a contractor's bid, include this in the contract. The contract should state X will receive the gift or rebate.
- "Lifetime guarantees" on building materials: These may not be enforceable by law.
- Exorbitant financing expenses: Dishonest contractors sometimes charge outrageous finance and interest fees.

Signing the Contract

Once you have selected a contractor, include all important terms in a written agreement.

- The contractor's name, address, license, and telephone number should appear in the contract.
- The starting date of the job and the expected time of completion must be stipulated. If time is of the essence, the agreement should state that all work must be completed by a definite date. Include a penalty if the job is not completed on time—for example, 20 percent reduction of the contract price. Be sure the contract

> *A couple was advanced $500 by a contractor to purchase aluminum siding and other improvements. After signing the contract, the couple discovered that they were obligated to pay 84 monthly installments, which totaled $4,000, for a $1,900 job. Always check your arithmetic and be aware of all hidden financing and interest expenses before accepting a home improvement loan from a building contractor.*

includes all the terms, duties, responsibilities, and conditions you discussed with the contractor. Under the Statute of Frauds, the law presumes that all discussions and oral agreements are incorporated into a written document; in most cases, judges will not hear testimony about what was agreed to orally when there is a written contract.

- Specify that the contractor must procure all permits required by law—certificates of insurance for workers' compensation, public liability, and property damage. Insist on copies of these permits 48 hours before work begins. The contract should also state that your deposit will be returned immediately if copies of these documents are not received.
- The contract should contain a detailed description of all materials to be used—include quantities, brand names, and model numbers. The contract should also specify that the materials to be used are *fully warranted,* that labor and materials are guaranteed against defect and poor workmanship, and that all defects will be corrected at no extra charge.
- Make sure there are no hidden charges in the contract that will increase the cost of the job. For example, the contractor agrees to move equipment and furniture back to its original location, clean up debris, post a performance bond, and return all unused materials to you at no additional cost.
- The manner of payment should be clearly spelled out. Keep the initial deposit as small as possible. Some states limit the down payment to 10 percent. Be sure payments are spaced to cover work

completed—that is, when 50 percent of the work is completed, no more than 50 percent of the payments should have been made.

- The method of financing should be clearly spelled out. Federal law requires that consumers be informed of all financing charges, the annual rate of interest expressed as a percent, the amount of each installment, the number of payments, and the penalties for late payment or default. Scrutinize all financing terms and figures.

- There must be a complete description of the actual work to be performed, and that work should comply with all applicable local, state, and national codes and standards.

- If specification sheets were given in the estimate, be sure the contract mentions that they are attached to the contract and made a part hereof.

- If the contract refers to plans, specify those plans in detail and mention that they are part of the contract attached hereto and incorporated herein.

- Specify what, if anything, you are doing yourself so as to avoid confusion.

- The contract should have a three-day cancellation notice. This is also called a "notice of right to rescission."

Make sure you understand everything in the contract before you sign.

- Make sure you understand everything in the contract before you sign. In fact, if the contract seems sophisticated or if large payments are involved, it may be wise to retain the services of a lawyer to review the contract and negotiate key terms on your behalf.

- Ask for an exact, signed copy. This may be either a carbon copy of the original or a photocopy, provided the contractor's *original* signature appears on your copy.

- Be sure a bona fide officer (president or vice president) of the company negotiates the deal and signs the agreement.

- Be sure the contract is complete and can be modified only in writing provided *both* parties sign a written amendment.

- Include a hold-back clause allowing you to retain a small amount of money, perhaps 10 percent of the contract price, to be paid only when the job is completed to your satisfaction.

- Consider inserting an arbitration clause to expedite the handling of disputes. Arbitration is a quick and inexpensive alternative to formal litigation (see Chapter 7). For example: "Any case or controversy arising as a result of this Agreement, among the parties to this Agreement or the subject matter hereto, shall be settled by arbitration in (location) under the then prevailing rules of the American Arbitration Association. The decision of the arbitrators shall be final and binding."

- Be sure that Truth-in-Lending language appears in the contract, setting forth your payments, the interest rate, the terms of the loan, and other details if the contractor or other source is financing the project for you. Be sure that the amounts are accurate.
- Pay by check to document the payment. If something goes wrong, you can stop payment. If you must pay by cash, get a signed receipt stating the amount you paid and what it was for.

Don't let the contractor or salesperson rush you into making a decision. *In many states, the law allows you to cancel the contract within a specified period* (typically three days) *for any reason without penalty.* Some states even require that a cancellation notice be attached to the contract. To find out about the applicable "cooling-off period" in your state, contact your nearest Better Business Bureau or attorney general's office for more details.

While the Job Is in Progress

There are several things you should do while the job is in progress. First, consider taking out extra insurance in case accidents happen to the contractor's employees or passersby. Then, remember to match payments to the progress of the job.

Finally, observe work to be sure the job is being done properly. Complain immediately about defective materials or shoddy workmanship. If you obtained financing through a lending institution, or are financing the job yourself, you may be able to withhold installments until the problems are corrected. Send a letter to the contractor stating the reasons for your dissatisfaction as well as clarifying what you contracted to receive and what you are now receiving (see Figure 2.3). Most contractors are anxious to receive final payment and will try to be accommodating if your demands aren't unreasonable.

After Job Completion

Consider the following points after the job is completed:

- Do not sign a completion certificate until the job has been completed.
- Insist that the Notice of Completion be filed in your county. This may ensure that your liability is at an end and that the waiting period has started in which suppliers, subcontractors, and others can file liens in the event of nonpayment. Since these notice periods usually extend for only 30 days, start the clock ticking.
- Do not make final payment until you are satisfied with the job and the contractor has provided you with releases from suppliers and persons employed on the job. Dishonest contractors sometimes pocket the money and fail to pay third parties, and the purchaser is often liable.
- Your local state's licensing board can verify the contractor's license and assist you in the event problems arise. If you have made final payment and are dissatisfied with the job, several options are available.

You can also send a formal written complaint to the local Department of Consumer Affairs, the BBB, the regional office of the FTC, or your state attorney general's office (see Figure 2.4). These agencies frequently conduct formal investigations. The advantage of filing a complaint with an appropriate agency is that it may not cost you anything to obtain satisfaction. For example, in some states the complaint division of the department of consumer affairs has the authority to schedule a hearing and impose penalties. These include fines, restitution, and orders requiring the contractor to complete the job in a satisfactory manner (or lose his or her license).

Along with your complaint, include copies (never originals) of all pertinent documents. This may include the contract, letters of protest, advertisements, guarantees, sales literature, and other correspondence. If possible, include photographs to demonstrate the current condition of the premises.

If you do not receive satisfaction through these agencies, you can sue the contractor in small claims court if the amount in dispute is under $2,000 or hire a lawyer and sue the contractor in a regular court.

Hiring an Architect

The same basic rules apply when hiring an architect as when hiring a contractor. Never hire an architect without first interviewing him or her. Examine the person's academic and professional experience and credentials. What professional associations does the architect belong to? Is he or she licensed, bonded, or registered with the department of education in your particular state? Some states require formal registration and testing to ensure competence.

Smart consumers always review samples of the architect's work. Obtain references and speak to people who had previously hired the architect. In addition to customers, this includes contractors, builders, landscapers, and planners who worked on job sites with the architect. If possible, look at the actual homes or offices.

Always ask for a written estimate of fees and compare several architects' fees before making your selection. In addition, request a written contract and make sure it contains the following provisions.

- All work will comply with existing federal, state, and local building codes and zoning laws. The architect will indemnify and hold you harmless from any losses caused by the negligence or omission of his or her work.
- Time is of the essence. The architect will prepare the drawings or plans within a specified time.
- You will be able to request reasonable modifications of the drawings or plans at little or no cost after receiving the initial set of plans.
- The architect will attend planning and zoning sessions on your behalf, if required, at little or no charge. Be sure you know how those charges will be computed.
- Full and final cost of the architect's work is specified.
- Full payment will not be required until satisfactory completion of the work.

If the contract is sophisticated or if a considerable fee is involved, it may be wise to retain the services of a lawyer familiar with architect law to review the agreement and negotiate additional terms on your behalf.

FIGURE 2.1 Sample Broker-Seller Agreement

Your Address
Telephone Number
Date

Name of Broker
ABC Brokerage Agency
Address

Dear (Name):

This will confirm that I agree to appoint you as my exclusive real estate broker effective (date) through (date).

You agree to use your best efforts to locate a willing, able, and ready purchaser for my home, located at (address).

It is agreed that the minimum acceptable price for my house will be $XXX. However, I have the right to withdraw my house from sale at any time, or to change the acceptable terms of sale.

For your services, you will be paid a commission of XX percent of the purchase price. However, you undertake your responsibilities with the understanding that your commission will not be earned until the full purchase price is paid to me. If this is not accomplished for any reason whatsoever, you will have no claim for commission or compensation in connection with this transaction.

As notice of your acceptance of this agreement, please countersign one copy of this letter and return it to me.

I look forward to working with you.

Sincerely,
(Signature)

Accepted and agreed to:
ABC Brokerage Agency

By:

[Send two copies certified mail, return receipt requested.]

FIGURE 2.2 Sample Letter of Protest Concerning Broker

Your Address
Telephone Number
Date

Regional Office of the National Association of Realtors
Address

Dear (Name of Directors),

Please treat this letter as a formal complaint against (name of realtor, address of firm).

(Describe dates and incidents in detail. For example:) I am an African-American. On July 27, 1993, (name of broker) showed my wife and me several houses for purchase. Despite our repeated requests, we were not shown any houses in (specify neighborhood). I believe we have been discriminated against, since the houses in the neighborhoods in which we desire to live are owned by nonminorities but we can afford them.

(State what you desire—e.g., commencement of an investigation, apology, action, etc. For example:) I would appreciate a formal letter of apology from (name of realtor), together with the name of another realtor who can help me locate a suitable house in my desired neighborhood for my family. Additionally, please conduct a formal investigation against (name of broker), advise me of the progress and disposition, and notify me of the outcome of your investigation. I also request that you make this letter a permanent part of (name of broker's) file. Feel free to contact me for further information or my participation at a formal hearing, if necessary.

If you do not conduct an investigation immediately, I shall consider filing a charge with the Equal Employment Opportunity Commission and taking other action as deemed appropriate. I hope that this shall not be necessary, and I thank you for your prompt attention and assistance in this matter.

Very truly yours,
(Signature)

cc: Regional Board of Realtors
Board of Consumer Affairs

[Send certified mail, return receipt requested.]

FIGURE 2.3 Sample Letter of Protest to Contractor

Your Address
Telephone Number
Date

Name of Contractor
Address

Dear (Name):

I hereby make a formal demand for you to cure the breach of our written agreement dated _____.

Our contract specifically states that "time is of the essence" and that you will finish the job (state what was agreed to) by (date).

You are now ten days late under the contract. Therefore, I demand (indicate what you want the contractor to do to remedy the situation—e.g., complete work immediately, reduce the final contract price, etc.).

Unless I hear from you immediately, I shall contact my attorney and file a formal complaint with the Department of Consumer Affairs.

Thank you for your cooperation in this matter.

Sincerely,
(Signature)

P.S. I am sending a copy of this letter to the Complaint Division of the Department of Consumer Affairs to remain on file.

[Send certified mail, return receipt requested.]

Most contractors are anxious to receive the final payment and will attempt to accommodate you if your demands are not unreasonable. Sending a letter should help.
(*Additional strategy:* Never agree to changes in the original contract unless the changes are agreed to in writing and initialed by both parties. This is for your protection.)

FIGURE 2.4 Sample Complaint Letter

Your Address
Telephone Number
Date

Director
Regional Office, Complaint Division
Department of Consumer Affairs
Address

Re: Request for Commencement of Investigation Against (Name of
  Contractor)

Dear (Name):

I hereby request you to commence a formal investigation of (name of contractor), located at (address), license number (#).

On (date), I signed a written contract with (name of contractor) to receive (specify work to be performed, where, at what price, etc.).

After the job was supposedly completed (state what happened, what you observed, etc.), I immediately contacted the contractor several times by phone and letter and requested that he complete the job in the manner specified in our contract. On (date), I spoke with (name) and (state what you told the contractor, whom you spoke with, what was said, etc.). On (date), I wrote a letter to the contractor.

To date I have been ignored.

I enclose a copy of the contract, color photographs showing the condition of the premises as they currently exist, and additional correspondence, including a formal demand letter which I sent by certified mail, return receipt requested, which went unanswered.

It is my understanding that you have the authority to schedule a hearing. I would appreciate that this be done as quickly as possible because (state the reason).

I am available at (give your telephone number) during business hours to assist you at your convenience. Kindly notify me of all developments in this matter.

Thank you for your cooperation and courtesies.

Very truly yours,
(Signature)

P.S. I am demanding (state how you have been damaged and what you wish to recover).

cc: Copy sent certified mail to contractor

[Send certified mail, return receipt requested.]

Wait a few days after sending the letter, then follow it up by calling the agency. If you do not receive appropriate action, consult a lawyer to determine your private legal rights and options.

3 Protecting Your Credit

Obtaining credit and maintaining a good credit rating are essential to financial success. Your life can be made miserable when financial institutions, credit card companies, and department stores (called "subscribers") or credit bureaus fail to update your credit reports or make mistakes regarding your credit history.

CREDIT RATINGS, CORRECTIONS, AND CARDS

The Federal Fair Credit Reporting Act

The following is a summary of what credit reporting bureaus can and cannot do under the federal Fair Credit Reporting Act:

- Credit reports cannot be furnished for illegitimate purposes or to people unauthorized to receive such reports.
- Reports cannot obtain information on judgments, tax liens, or arrest records more than seven years old except when the person requesting the information is considering extending credit or providing insurance of more than $50,000 or offering employment for a job paying more than $20,000. Past bankruptcies may be reported up to 10 years.

- Once notified that a report is inaccurate, all reasonable requests must be investigated and false information corrected.
- Any company or person who asks for an investigative report on you must promptly notify you in writing. You may receive a copy of the final report, but you must ask for it in writing.
- Any company that turns you down for credit, insurance, or employment partly because of information contained in a consumer credit report must supply the name and address of the agency that furnished the report.
- At your request, a reporting agency must clearly and accurately disclose the source, nature, and substance of all information it has on you in its files.

Repairing Bad Credit

There are simple steps you can take to remedy poor credit without the assistance of a credit agency or attorney. The basic aim is to find out what in your credit file is being reported to others, correct or delete inaccurate or incomplete information, and, if necessary, have an agency renotify recipients of reports.

1. Request a credit report once a year from a major credit bureau to be certain that it is accurate and that no adverse credit reports have been reported by mistake. Contact a major credit reporting agency whenever you discover a problem. These companies have local offices in major cities and are listed in the telephone directory.

   Depending on the circumstances, you may not be charged for your credit report. TRW Information Service will give consumers a free copy of the credit report once a year (beyond that, it's $7.50 each time the report is furnished). Send a letter to TRW Consumer Assistance, P.O. Box 2350, Chatsworth, CA 91313-2350. The letter must contain your full name with middle initials and generational indicators, such as Jr. and Sr.; if married, include your spouse's first name. It should also include your current and previous addresses with zip codes, social security number, date of birth, and a photocopy of a driver's license or recent telephone or

> *Gwen applied for a revolving credit bank loan but was turned down. The bank advised her in writing that a TRW Information Service report (one of the nation's biggest credit reporting companies) did not justify the risk because a tax lien had been filed in her city last year due to a failure to pay unincorporated business tax. Gwen had, in fact, properly paid all taxes due. She contacted the city to investigate and remedy the mistake and eventually had the unfavorable comment removed from her credit record.*

utility bill. Be sure to include the address where the report should be sent. You should receive it within about three weeks.

Other agencies may charge you a fee (typically under $25), but if you have been denied credit on the basis of the report within the previous 30 days, the charge must be waived. The major credit bureaus also have additional services you can purchase for a fee, including credit tips, increased access to your credit reports, analysis of your financial standing, and easier-to-read versions of the credit report (see page 81 for agency addresses).

Anytime you apply for a loan or credit and are rejected, the institution that rejected your request must provide written notice of the rejection along with the reason given by the credit bureau as a basis for the rejection.

2. Demand, in writing, an explanation of the discrepancy and request a complete report of your credit history. The law requires that a credit bureau inform you of what is contained in your credit report upon request. It does not have to show you the actual report (but most do).

3. You can contact the subscriber directly to discuss why your credit is being impaired. For example, you can visit the local department store that claims you failed to pay your bill and bring along the canceled check to prove the store is wrong. Even if the dispute is valid, you may be able to obtain satisfaction by arranging a settlement on the unpaid account to clear up the problem.

You can also ask your credit card company to suspend your

credit for a designated period until payments are made. This may prevent negative items from being generated on your account, and it may avoid the cancellation of your credit card.

4. If you find any errors in your report, notify the bureau in writing immediately. Identify the error and demand a prompt investigation and deletion or correction. The letter should also state that an error or discrepancy is causing *injury* to your credit rating. The Fair Credit Reporting Act allows bureaus to ignore investigating requests deemed frivolous or unworthy of scrutiny. More than 50 percent of disputed or negative items are deleted from reports when consumers initiate inquiries. Also instruct the bureau not to divulge your credit history to unauthorized entities (you must sign an authorization form). Unauthorized credit checks are illegal.

More than 50 percent of negative items are deleted from credit reports when consumers initiate inquiries.

5. The bureau has 30 days to investigate and act on your complaint. During this time it typically contacts subscribers to verify charges incurred against your account; if a subscriber does not respond to the bureau's inquiry, the disputed item is supposed to be deleted automatically from your account. If you fail to receive a prompt response, send a follow-up letter demanding that an accurate report be generated or that the disputed item be deleted from your credit report.

6. You can also make an appointment to visit your local credit bureau. A representative from the credit agency must agree to see you if you have been denied credit within the last 30 days and have proof, such as a photocopy of the denial letter. Dealing with the agency in person often speeds up the process.

7. If the bureau insists that your claim is frivolous or fails to respond properly, it will be necessary to contact the regional office of the FTC, the regulatory agency empowered to oversee credit bureaus. Or you can sue the bureau under the guidelines contained in the Fair Credit Reporting Act.

8. Finally, even if a credit bureau refuses to correct your report, you have the right to enter a statement of 100 words or less in your file explaining why the record is inaccurate. The reporting company

> *One individual won $10,000 in punitive damages and $8,000 in legal fees after proving that he tried many times in good faith to correct errors in his report to no avail and that his credit suffered as a result.*

must include your statement in any reports it issues on you. It is also possible to add favorable information to your credit report, such as added outside income. Some credit bureaus charge a slight fee for adding favorable items, but it can help repair your credit picture (see Figures 3.1, 3.2, and 3.3).

LARGEST CREDIT REPORTING BUREAUS

TRW Credit Information Services
500 City Parkway West
Orange, CA 92667

TRW Information Services
Attention: Consumer Assistance
P.O. Box 749029
Dallas, TX 75374-9029
(214) 235-1200, ext. 251

CBI/EQUIFAX
P.O. Box 740241
Atlanta, GA 30375-0241
(404) 885-8000

Trans Union Credit Information
111 West Jackson Boulevard
Chicago, IL 60604

Chelton Creditmatic Systems
12606 Greenville Avenue
Dallas, TX 75243

Associated Credit Services, Inc.
652 East North Belt, Suite 400
Houston, TX 77060

Final Strategies to Improve Your Credit

- There are credit-counseling agencies, credit-cleaning agencies, and consultants who, for a fee, claim to be able to improve your credit and teach you how to investigate and resolve disputes on your behalf. There are also nonprofit consumer credit–counseling agencies, which are widespread and honest. If you cannot locate such an agency and are considering hiring a consultant for a fee, be sure that such a person or business demonstrates his or her credentials and that you are not overbilled. For maximum protection, consider hiring a certified public accountant, attorney, or similar professional and that a written agreement be furnished to you in advance disclosing the maximum amount of fees and costs to be charged and what will be accomplished. If possible, personally interview and ask for references before paying fees.

- More than 50 percent of all negative information is often removed from a credit file following the first verification inquiry letter, so take action immediately. In many situations, the elimination of these errors alone may immediately change you from a negative credit risk to a positive one.

- Be persistent. Department stores and other businesses want your business and goodwill and may be inclined to change your credit history or eliminate the transaction under dispute if you are persuasive and courteous.

- Loan and credit institutions use a job classification system in determining and establishing a credit background. For example, companies are more inclined to extend credit to teachers than to actors. If there is a different way to list your job classification or verify longer, permanent employment, it may be a good idea to do so provided *no material misstatements* are included.

- Visa or MasterCard members with poor credit can often obtain "instant credit" from department stores that issue their own credit cards. Then, when you charge a purchase and make a timely payment, you may have enhanced your credit rating even though your older record may not be favorable.

- You may be able to improve your credit history by asking a subscriber with whom you have a favorable relationship to contact a credit bureau and record this relationship on your account.

- Compare your credit report with your records at least once a year to monitor any problems or inconsistencies and stop potential problems before your credit reputation is impaired.

- If you are having a temporary problem paying your bills, consider paying off all small bills first. You may be able to keep a positive credit history by eliminating a lot of creditors. Also, larger creditors often do not report arrears for several months, so you may be able to buy some time and not have your credit rating impaired.

- Recognize that women sometimes unfairly encounter credit problems, particularly older married women. Fortunately, the federal Equal Credit Opportunity Act gave women protection from credit discrimination. However, if you were married before 1977 (when the law was enacted), your credit activities may still be reflected in your husband's report and it may be difficult or impossible to obtain credit in your own name.

  To increase the chances of establishing your own credit, it is suggested that you:
  - •• open a bank account in your own name
  - •• ask that all credit be reported in your complete name (i.e., "Gwen Smith," not "Mrs. Steven Smith")
  - •• obtain one credit card and several store charge cards in your own name and not your husband's name
  - •• consider building a separate credit identity using your maiden name where warranted
  - •• consider applying for a "secured" credit card if you have difficulty qualifying for a regular credit card because you lack a credit history. Although these cards look and spend like other charge cards, they differ from conventional cards because holders are required to deposit an amount in a bank account at least equal to the amount of their card's credit limit. Bankcard Holders of America, located at 560 Herndon Parkway, Suite 120, Herndon, Virginia 22070, provides additional information about banks offering secured credit cards. The fee is $4.
  - •• attempt to have a parent or relative cosign and assume responsibility for any debts you incur in order to help you initially qualify for a credit card. Once you establish your creditworthiness and a good credit history, you will then have no problem getting other cards (of a type of your choosing) on your own.
- Finally, understand that there is no guarantee to a favorable credit rating, particularly in instances where:
  - •• no credit file has been established

•• you previously filed for bankruptcy protection or had your
wages garnished, assets repossessed or attached, or were found
guilty of delinquent child support

•• you recently moved or you are unable to verify employment,
income, furnish credit references, or adequately complete credit
applications

Consumer-related credit fraud is on the rise. Numerous scams are popular, including loan brokers and "professionals" who take cash payments from customers needing jobs or those having poor credit desiring to buy homes or facing mortgage foreclosures. Unfortunately, most of these people promise to help but do nothing.

> *One advance-fee loan operation was the subject of hundreds of complaints from consumers from out of state. The company solicited through classified ads and telemarketing and persuaded consumers with poor credit to send between $200 and $800 for guaranteed loans that never materialized. Postal inspectors eventually brought charges against the principals and seized their assets.*

Other tips to avoid related credit fraud include:

• Avoid using loan brokers or other credit professionals who
demand a fee in advance.
• Use 900 numbers with caution, since even a single call could cost
you more than $100.
• Since dubious credit and mortgage fixers, loan brokers, and job
finders flourish in times of economic recession, be wary of
individuals and firms you have never heard about or can't receive
favorable references about.
• Always inquire about an individual's or a firm's reputation by
contacting your local Better Business Bureau or consumer
protection agency to discover whether any complaints have been
previously filed.

Credit Card Problems

There are many types of charge cards, including credit cards, travel and entertainment cards, bank credit cards, premium cards, and secured credit cards. Each offers different advantages, costs, and billing practices. When shopping for charge cards, weigh these factors:

- interest rate
- annual fee
- acceptance by merchants
- grace periods before payment is required or penalties imposed
- availability of cash advances
- fringe benefits, including flight insurance, collision coverage on rental cars, telephone and travel discounts

If your card is lost or stolen, report this within 24 hours so you will not be responsible for unauthorized charges in excess of $50 per card. Although loss of a card may do you no major financial harm, it can interfere with your credit if you do not report the loss immediately.

If your credit card is lost or stolen, report this within 24 hours.

Never lend your card, do not disclose your account number over the telephone to anyone you do not know, and check all statements promptly for unauthorized transactions.

Billing Errors

The Fair Credit Billing Act of 1974 offers significant protection against billing errors made by the card issuer or the merchant. Billing errors for which the issuing bank is responsible include failure to record payments that you made and mathematical errors in totaling your charges or calculating the finance charge.

Billing errors for which merchants are responsible include charges for items you did not order or never received; items delivered to the wrong address, in the wrong quantity, or so much later than promised that the bill arrived before the item; and items that turned out to be different from what you ordered.

When you discover an error, notify the issuing bank *in writing* within

60 days of receiving the statement. Your letter should include your account number, a description of the error, the amount of the error, and, if possible, some explanation of why the error may have occurred. If the error involves a merchant, attach copies of bills, sales receipts, or other supporting documents.

While the dispute is pending, you may withhold payment of the disputed amount, but you must pay the rest of your balance. During this time, the card issuer may not close your account or threaten your credit rating by reporting you as delinquent.

The card issuer must respond to your letter within 30 days and must, within 90 days, investigate your complaint. If your claim turns out to be justified, the charge is canceled; if not, you must pay the amount plus any interest charges that have accrued.

Problems with Banks

Common financial problems include:

- failure of banks to specify adequate reasons for denying credit
- electronic fund and other account mix-ups
- imposition of unwarranted fees
- bank credit card errors
- misrepresentation of credit charges, such as not disclosing the annual percentage rates on loans
- discriminatory lending decisions on the basis of race, gender, age, marital status, national origin, religion, or because the applicant is on welfare or in the past has complained about the bank

You should first attempt to resolve the problem directly with the bank. Discuss the problem in person if necessary, and follow up all meetings with a letter confirming the substance of the meeting and what you were promised, such as immediate action. (Always send the letters by certified mail, return receipt requested, so you can prove delivery.)

If the matter is not resolved quickly, appeal to a supervisor or officer of the bank. Send a final letter warning that you will take legal action if the problem is not solved.

Finally, you can hire a lawyer to take further action on your behalf. There are also agencies established to oversee, regulate, and handle complaints against banks in their jurisdiction. These include your state's banking department, Federal Home Loan Bank, U.S. Comptroller of the Currency, Federal Reserve Bank, and Federal Deposit Insurance Corporation.

If you have trouble reaching the appropriate agency, contact your regional or local department of consumer affairs as a last resort. Most consumer affairs agencies will intervene on a consumer's behalf or can guide you in this area.

COLLECTION AGENCY HARASSMENT

Retail establishments employ various tactics to collect delinquent payments. The methods used depend on the store's size and business policy. Most stores attempt to collect the debt either directly or through an attorney. Many, however, utilize the services of collection agencies.

Although the majority of collection agencies follow acceptable collection practices, the debt collection area continues to be a principal source of consumer complaints.

The most common abuses are persistent telephone calls at inconvenient hours and threatening letters and telegrams, including phony legal subpoenas. Collectors frequently pretend they are collection-reporting services as well as collection agencies and claim they can list unpaid accounts with various merchant credit retail associations. Thus, people are incorrectly led to believe that their credit rating will be seriously affected unless the bill is promptly paid. Also, some agencies illegally tack collection charges onto the debt.

Congress expanded the rights of consumers by enacting the Fair Debt Collection Practices Act more than a decade ago. Collection agencies are forbidden from repeatedly calling you at home or sending you threaten-

---

The mother of a debtor received a telephone call at her home from a collector who identified herself as a hospital employee. The woman was told that her grandchildren had been involved in an automobile accident. This was done merely to obtain her son's home address and telephone number.

ing letters. Nor are they allowed to continuously contact your neighbors, relatives, and employers. The law enables you to sue debt collectors who employ false representations, unfair practices, and abuse while trying to enforce a debt. Any collection agency that fails to comply with the act's provisions is liable for actual damages, statutory damages up to $1,000, and attorney's costs.

When Does the Law Apply?

The law protects you against abusive practices of private collection agencies, professional collectors in the business of collecting debts for banks, and companies that service mortgage loans. It does *not* apply to attorneys, federal employees, and in-house collectors.

There are several exceptions. For example, if you buy a television set from Bad Bernie's (BB) Appliance Store on credit, and BB has its own credit department to collect payments, that department is an in-house collector and cannot be sued under the Fair Debt Collection Practices Act. However, BB *can* be sued if: BB's credit department collects money for BB under a different name, BB employees mail collection letters on the personal stationery of an attorney who plays only a small role in the collection process, or BB sends out collection letters on the agency's letterhead, even though the letter states that all payments are to be sent directly to BB.

What Collectors Cannot Do

Debt collectors cannot use obscene language or publish "shame" lists of people who allegedly refuse to pay their debts. Collectors cannot misrepresent themselves as attorneys or as associated with a government or law enforcement agency. They cannot threaten you, your property, or your reputation. For example, letters stating "It may be necessary for our agent to call on you personally" or "A copy of this letter is being sent to an attorney, instructing him to bring you in for an oral examination and attach your personal property" are forbidden. In addition, threats of arrest or wage garnishment for nonpayment (when not allowed by local law), or threats to take legal action that collectors never intend to pursue, give you a legal basis to sue.

A favorite collection tactic is to send ornamented collection letters with official-looking seals. These convey the impression that they are legal documents issued by a court. A popular version states "The Within-named Creditor under State Statutes and Provisions hereby makes final demand for nonpayment of indebtedness." Letters of this sort and those that pretend to offer legal advice—for example, stating "In our judg-ment"—are not allowed, nor are notices demanding that the debtor appear at collection agency offices.

Collectors sometimes charge telegram fees and reverse telephone charges before revealing the purpose of the communication. The law pro-tects you from these practices. In addition, late charges, interest, collec-tion fees, and expenses cannot be added to the amount of money owed unless this is permitted under state law and you originally agreed *in writ-ing* to such an arrangement before a purchase was made.

The law restricts the frequency and time of day when you can be con-tacted. No communication to you or your family is allowed before 8:00 A.M. or after 9:00 P.M. You cannot be called at work if the collector is told that the employer forbids personal phone calls. Letters can no longer be sent to an employer, asking him or her to discuss the debt with you. In addition, once you hire a lawyer, contact can only be made through your lawyer, unless he or she allows the collection agency to communi-cate with you.

Collection Agency Efforts to Find You

Collection agencies may try to locate you through a third person, pro-vided the information sought includes only a home address, telephone number, or business address. Relatives and neighbors have been the target of ploys to obtain this information. Prizes, gifts, and rewards have been offered but never given. These practices are now illegal. Although com-munications can be made by mail, telephone, or personal visits, debt col-lectors must:

- identify themselves—giving the true name of their collection agency upon request—and say that they are seeking to acquire or confirm location information
- contact the third party only once unless the information received is

incorrect or they are given permission by that person to call back for more information

- never voluntarily state that they work for a collection agency or that they are making this communication because a debt is owed

In addition, the FTC, which enforces the Fair Debt Collection Practices Act, forbids the suggestion of collection conveyed through the mail. The mere use of language on a postcard or letter indicating debt collection, such as the name General Credit Control, Inc., in the return address or on the back of an envelope, violates the law. This ensures that the debtor's relatives and neighbors do not learn of his or her financial condition.

What to Do If You Are Contacted

Many people are willing to pay their debts but need additional time to do so. The law addresses this problem. Once you are contacted by a collection agency, request verification of the debt. The agency is required to tell you the amount of the debt and the name and address of the original creditor. Then you have the right to dispute the debt. During a dispute, all collection agency activity must stop until:

- the agency contacts the creditor to determine if the debt is correct, or
- the agency sends you written notification about the debt

Therefore, if you need more time to ready your finances, and the collection agency threatens to sue unless payment is made immediately, send a letter to the agency, requesting written verification of the debt (see Figure 3.4). This will effectively stall agency action for some time.

Getting the Collection Agency Off Your Back

One of the most important features of the Fair Debt Collection Practices Act is that it protects your right to be left alone. Even if you legitimately owe a debt, you can notify the agency in writing to stop all further contact and *this request must be honored.* You can exercise this right before or after you request written verification of the debt.

The agency cannot contact you, except by letter, stating that all collection efforts are being stopped or that specific legal action to recover the debt has been started. It is that simple.

The agency's only alternative may be litigation. However, persons with small debts, who forbid collection agencies to contact them, often have their debts "wiped out" since the amount of money owed doesn't justify the time and expense of a lawsuit. Keep in mind that your credit rating may be impaired by the failure to pay a legitimate debt.

How to Remedy Abuses

Save all letters, telegrams, and other written documents. Collect sworn affidavits from friends, neighbors, and employers who have been contacted by the collection agency. If you are unable to sleep, or suffer a physical ailment such as nausea or weight loss as a result of harassment, document all doctor visits, medical reports, bills, and prescription purchases. Some people even tape record phone conversations in order to obtain documented proof of wrongful acts (if you wish to do this, consult a lawyer because in some states taping a conversation without the other person's permission is illegal).

Speak to a lawyer after collecting your information. He or she will decide whether to sue the collection agency under state law, the Fair Debt Collection Practices Act, or contact the FTC. If suit is brought under the Fair Debt Collection Act, it must be filed within one year.

If you prove your case, the court will order the collection agency to reimburse you for legal fees and court costs. The court can also award money for mental anguish caused by repetitious phone calls at all hours. You can even recover money spent for medical treatment, as well as lost wages, provided the collector's calls caused this condition. Punitive damages for vindictive behavior may also be awarded.

Consult the law in your state to determine whether the state imposes stronger penalties than federal law. If so, file your lawsuit in state court.

There is one final alternative. A violation of the Fair Debt Collection Practices Act is considered an unfair and deceptive practice. Thus, contact the FTC if you believe you are the victim of harassment (see Figure 3.5). The FTC can impose a variety of sanctions on a collection agency, including the return of money or property, fines, and a public announcement of wrongdoing.

> *Recently, the FTC entered into a consent judgment with a large collection agency accused of telephone harassment, illegal third-party contacts, and false threats of civil and criminal process. The agency agreed to pay $90,000 in civil penalties and other relief. Another $65,000 penalty was obtained from a firm that overcharged debtors. The money was used to refund the overcharges.*

Summary of Steps to Limit Collection Abuse

Never:

- disclose an unlisted telephone number on a credit application
- sign retail establishment contracts that authorize additional charges and permit collectors to contact whomever they wish about the debt
- accept collect calls from collection agencies
- volunteer information about your finances
- sign postdated checks to demonstrate good faith
- be intimidated by collectors

Always:

- assert your rights
- send correspondence by certified mail, return receipt requested
- inquire whether interest and collection charges have illegally been added to the principal debt
- instruct collectors not to call you at work because your employer forbids personal phone calls
- instruct the collector to apply payment to a *specific* debt if more than one debt is owed
- attempt to resolve debts
- contact the Federal Trade Commission, your state attorney general's office, or a local consumer protection agency if you are harassed

FIGURE 3.1 Sample Letter to a Credit-Reporting Agency

Your Address
Telephone Number
Social Security Number
Date

Reporting Agency
Address

To Whom It May Concern:

On (date) I was notified by (specify) that my application for credit had been rejected. Enclosed is a copy of the notice.

Pursuant to the Fair Credit Reporting Act, please immediately send me a copy of my present credit file and summary history. I understand that there will be no charge for this service.

Since my credit is being wrongly impaired and time is of the essence in correcting any inaccurate or incomplete information that may be contained in my file, I request that you promptly provide me with the report so that corrective action may be taken. This can be done via a telephone appointment if you prefer, and I thank you for your prompt attention and assistance in this matter.

Very truly yours,
(Signature)

[Send certified mail, return receipt requested.]

FIGURE 3.2 Sample Letter Requesting Information Concerning an Investigative Report

---

Your Address
Telephone Number
Date

Company Requesting Report
Address

To Whom It May Concern:

    Thank you for your letter of (date) notifying me that you were requesting my consumer credit history from (specify).

    Please advise me in writing why you have requested such information. In addition, I expect to receive a copy of the report so that I can correct any incorrect information.

    Your cooperation is greatly appreciated.

Very truly yours,
(Signature)

[Send certified mail, return receipt requested.]

FIGURE 3.3 Sample Letter Disputing Information in Your Credit File

---

Your Address
Telephone Number
Date

Credit Bureau
Address

To Whom It May Concern:

On (date) I received a copy of my credit history, enclosed, which contained inaccuracies that are severely affecting my credit. The following items are incorrect: (specify reported items and why they are incorrect).

Please promptly investigate these items and make the necessary corrections. Furthermore, please notify (name of subscriber or company seeking information or turning you down for credit) immediately of the corrections.

Feel free to get in touch with me at the above address if you need further information. Thank you.

Very truly yours,
(Signature)

[Send certified mail, return receipt requested.]

FIGURE 3.4 Sample Letter Requesting Verification of Debt

Your Name
Address
Date

Name
Title
ABC Collection Agency
Address

Re: Request for written verification of my disputed debt with (name of creditor)

Dear (Name):

On (date), you contacted me by (letter, phone, telegram, in person) concerning a purported debt I owe to (name of creditor).

I do not owe such a debt because (billing error, merchandise returned, merchandise damaged, merchandise unsatisfactory).

I will be contacting (name of creditor) in an effort to resolve this matter. In the meantime please:

1. Verify the amount of the alleged debt with (name of creditor).
2. Send me a copy of the written verification.
3. Stop all collection efforts until I receive a copy of this written verification.

Thank you for your cooperation.

Very truly yours,
(Signature)

cc: creditor

[Send certified mail, return receipt requested.]

FIGURE 3.5 Sample Letter Protesting Credit Harassment

Your Name
Address
Date

Director
Regional Office
Federal Trade Commission
(Address)

Re: Violation by (name of agency) of the Fair Debt Collection Practices
    Act

Dear (Name):

I am writing to you regarding the unfair practices of (name of agency) located at (address).

On (dates) I was harassed by said agency (explain how). This arose out of a disputed debt with (name of creditor).

I (state what you told the agency, whom you spoke with, and why your requests have not been honored).

I enclose copies of correspondence with (name of agency). I would appreciate it if you would look into this matter to eliminate such outrageous conduct.

You can reach me at the above address if you need further information. Please notify me of all developments in this matter.

Thank you for your cooperation.

Very truly yours,
(Signature)

cc: collection agency, creditor

[Send certified mail, return receipt requested.]

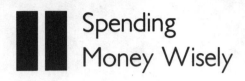

Spending
Money Wisely

4 Safeguarding Product Purchases

AUTOMOBILE WARRANTIES, LEMON LAWS, AND SERVICE RIP-OFFS

At least two manufacturing defects are found in the average new car within the first 90 days after purchase. Although manufacturers' warranties are designed to correct these problems—free—during the warranty period, consumers are often dissatisfied with the warranty process. This stems primarily from a dealer's failure to cooperate in working on the repairs or in successfully repairing the defect.

Also, most manufacturers do not sell new cars with full warranties but only with warranties for specific parts for a limited duration.

Most manufacturers do not sell new cars with full warranties but only with warranties for specific parts for a limited duration.

Dealers for most car makers are required to perform repairs covered by warranty for all cars of that make no matter where the car was purchased. The more obvious the defect and the easier it is to fix, the less resistance you're likely to encounter from the dealer. For example, it's hard for the service manager to argue that dangling wires are normal. If it's a judgment call, however, watch out. A distorted windshield may look "just fine" to the service manager.

Warranty work is often less lucrative for the dealer than ordinary repairs, since the factory may not pay the dealer for time spent diagnosing a problem or for clean-up. Nor does the factory pay for minor adjustments. However, that's the dealer's problem, not yours.

> *Mary noticed a problem with her brakes less than 90 days after she bought a new car. Whenever it rained and she applied the brakes hard, she heard a sharp piercing noise. Mary visited the dealership where she bought the car and complained about the problem. She took along a friend to confirm the problem and to witness the dealer's response. The car was repaired under warranty, and the problem was corrected within two days at no charge for parts, labor, or service. Additionally, Mary requested and was given a replacement car for the two days the car was being inspected and serviced.*

If you have difficulty obtaining satisfaction under your warranty, follow these steps:

1. If the dealer refuses to make a needed warranty repair without charge, call the nearest factory zone manager listed in your owner's manual. Ask for a representative to meet with you and the dealer's service manager. If the problem affects safety, have the repair made *immediately,* even if you have to pay, and argue about the refund later.
2. If you don't get satisfaction from the zone office, send a certified letter to the manufacturer's headquarters or main office (or, with an import, to the distributor). Describe the problem briefly; explain what the dealer has offered and what you think should be done.
3. If the letter fails to get results, consider suing the dealer or automaker in small claims court or through your state's lemon law arbitration proceeding or Better Business Bureau (see Chapter 7).

"SECRET WARRANTIES"

A secret warranty is a manufacturer's warranty extended beyond the initial warranty period to cover all or part of a specific repair when a component has a high failure rate. It's a secret because the automaker doesn't notify car owners of the extended coverage but merely makes it available to those in the know.

If you think your car troubles might be the result of a defect, first contact your dealer's service manager or customer-service representative. Keep all records of repair work done on your car. If you don't get satisfaction, contact the nearest factory regional office or the manufacturer's home office.

To get information on secret warranties, write to the Center for Auto Safety, 2001 S Street NW, Washington, D.C. 20009. The center is a clearinghouse for automotive complaints. By cataloging owners' complaints concerning different car models, buttressed with information provided by the automakers' own dealer service bulletins, the center can tell you if your car's troubles are commonplace and if they are eligible for free repair by the dealer.

Inquiries to the center should include a self-addressed stamped envelope; the make, model, and year of your car; and a description of the specific problem you're experiencing.

Lemon Laws

In most states, legislation called "lemon laws" attempts to assure consumers of a refund or replacement when the manufacturer is unable, within a reasonable time, to remedy a substantial defect. Used in conjunction with private arbitration as a dispute resolution mechanism, these laws have helped some consumers receive relatively quick, inexpensive, and informal relief.

Some of the key features of lemon laws include offering state-certified or state-sponsored dispute resolution, expanding the scope to include leased and used vehicles, increasing the length of the warranty coverage, and reducing the number of repair attempts that qualify a vehicle as a lemon. Some laws also cover commercial vehicles, trucks, and motorcycles. To understand the limits and extent of protection, check your state law.

Arbitration

The majority of state lemon laws force consumers to use the manufacturer's informal dispute resolution mechanism before proceeding to court. These include the Ford Consumer Appeals Board, Chrysler Customer Satisfaction Arbitration Board, Better Business Bureau (BBB) AUTOLINE, and National Automobile Dealers Association AUTOCAP. If you prevail, you will usually be entitled to a refund of the purchase price or a replacement vehicle. (Attorney fees are specifically provided in most states.)

To begin the process, file a form to describe the problem. Your automobile dealer then comments and/or defends the charges in writing. After you have notified the manufacturer of the problem covered by the lemon laws, he or she must make reasonable attempts under particular state laws to repair the vehicle within reasonable limits.

Boards are made up of one or more arbitrators who base their decisions on written statements from the parties involved, testimony at hearings, and physical inspection of the auto. It takes about two months from the date a complaint is received to the date a decision is rendered. The average cost is around $350. Finally, most states allow consumers to file private lawsuits if they are unable to resolve the matter through arbitration. If you cannot afford a private lawyer, speak to your local legal referral service or Legal Aid Society or contact your local Better Business Bureau or state attorney general's office for help.

How to Win in Arbitration

1. Choose the proper avenue of arbitration. Dealer arbitrations, such as the Ford or Chrysler programs, are available. In

AUTOCAP arbitration, you can usually speak directly to an arbitrator (who may try to settle your matter before the hearing). The BBB AUTOLINE is an alternative.

2. Carefully read all the information on whatever arbitration program you select. You can get literature from your dealer, manufacturer, or your local BBB or department of consumer affairs. The BBB can answer questions and provide an arbitration agreement that states how the arbitration will proceed and what will be heard. Sometimes the BBB helps prepare your case and discuss your options. For example, do you want a refund or a comparable replacement vehicle? An in-person hearing or only a written presentation? Where do you want the hearing to be conducted? They can also show you how to fill out the forms properly (vehicle identification number, description of defect, redress sought, and so on).

3. Prepare for arbitration. To prove your purchase and damages, you have to submit:
   - the contract of purchase and/or financing agreement
   - the amount of your down payment and number of payments made
   - documentation of all attempted repairs within the time period designated in your state's lemon law
   - routine and warranty maintenance previously performed (to show that the car was not misused)
   - your warranty contract (if any)
   - service bulletins that list defects that are under warranty (Be sure to request these.)
   - any other correspondence to help your case

   Organize this information chronologically. Present all records indicating whom you spoke with about the defect, when and where, and make copies of all letters of protest sent.

4. Have witnesses testify on your behalf. You can present signed and notarized affidavits or request that the witness accompany you to the arbitration (this is usually better). If an important witness, such as a neutral mechanic who examined repeated repair attempts, refuses to go, he or she may be subpoenaed by the arbitrator. You will probably have to give the opposing side the names of all witnesses you intend to call to avoid surprises.

5. Be businesslike. Present your case directly, and answer all questions. Almost any kind of evidence can be presented provided it directly pertains to your case. Do not overburden the arbitrator with emotional rhetoric.
6. Attend all prehearings with the opposition. This can help you size up your opponent, and you may be able to agree on certain parameters before the hearing, such as procedural points.
7. Know the major provisions of your state's lemon law. These laws define language such as "reasonable opportunity to repair." Knowing the technical aspects of the law will help you respond when the opposition claims it honored its side of the bargain.
8. You can amend your presentation even after initiation of the case. For example, you have the right to review all the materials presented by the other side, clarify points, and respond to ambiguous statements for the record.
9. If you feel the arbitration was mishandled or that incorrect information regarding your particular arbitration program was furnished to you, contact your local consumer's protection bureau or the FTC for advice.
10. Speak to an attorney if necessary. You can retain the services of a knowledgeable attorney to assist you in all informal and formal stages of the arbitration if desired.

Used Cars

The best way to predict performance of a used car is to know how it was treated and what problems it has had. Therefore, a friend is the best source for a used car.

On the other hand, if you buy a used car from a new-car dealer, you will probably pay more but have a wider selection. You may also be able to obtain written warranties and access to service facilities. If possible, buy a used car of the same brand as the new cars the dealer sells. That way it is easier to obtain parts and you can expect better servicing.

The best way to predict performance of a used car is to know how it was treated and what problems it has had.

Cars sold by used-car dealers are usually cheaper, but many sell cars "as is," with no warranties or extremely limited warranties. (For a specific price for a specific used-car model, call Consumer Reports Used Car Price Service [1-900-446-1120]. The service costs $1.75 per minute— expect to spend five or more minutes for a typical call.) Also, used-car dealers rarely know the history of these cars, since they often obtain them at auctions and foreclosures. And they rarely have on-site repair facilities.

Watch for cars purchased from taxi companies or police departments; they often have excessive wear. If possible, buy a used car from a dealership that has been in business for a long time; it may have a better reputation and make good on promises.

If you buy from a used-car rental company, try to obtain the complete maintenance history of the car and buy a relatively new model. On the down side, however, rental cars often have very high mileage.

Be careful when buying a car from a private seller you don't know. Consumers often think they are buying a car from a private individual but, in fact, they may be buying from a pro masquerading as a private seller. Always ask to see the title of the car; if the name on the title and the seller's name don't match, ask why.

Odometer Fraud

More than half of all used cars have odometers that have been rolled back. Although federal and state laws make it a crime to disconnect, alter, or reset the odometer, the problem is a common one.

- Examine maintenance stickers on the doorpost or air filter. Mileage is sometimes noted when maintenance is performed.
- Examine wear on the clutch, brake, and accelerator pedals and look for excessive scratches on the ignition lock. Cars with fewer than 30,000 miles should not show excessive wear on these items.
- Check the dashboard for missing screws and make sure all the numbers on the odometer line up properly.
- Check the name on the title. It should be the seller's, previous owner's, or dealer's name. Be suspicious of titles with out-of-state addresses, post office boxes, or auction company names.
- Study all numbers on the title. Disreputable sellers often obscure the numbers with official-looking stamps or staple or fold the title through the middle of the odometer reading or vehicle number.

- Ask your mechanic to inspect the engine compression and look for transmission problems and worn struts or ball joints.

Warranties

Since most used cars are sold as is, it is important to try to obtain a full or limited warranty. You have a better chance of obtaining a limited warranty when buying a used car from a car rental company or new-car dealer.

Under federal law, used-car dealers selling more than six cars in a 12-month period must specify what warranties go with the car and post this conspicuously on the car. Read the warranty carefully, and question any ambiguous or confusing language. Try to get the longest and best warranty possible, such as on cost for replaced parts or repairs within the first six months of purchase or 5,000 miles driven. Negotiate for a reduced price if you do not receive a full warranty or acceptable terms. Insist that the warranty be incorporated into the final contract of sale.

Dealers

1. Negotiate with licensed dealers only.
2. Inspect the vehicle's internal and external features. Make the inspection during the day when there is adequate light. Test drive the car, preferably alone, and listen for odd noises and other irregularities.
3. Have the car inspected by your regular mechanic or diagnostic center. Never buy a car from a seller who won't allow an independent inspection.
4. Discuss key points.
   - What is the price of the car? Are tax, dealer preparation, and transportation included?
   - What are the terms of payment?
   - What are the financing charges for installment payments?
   - Will you receive a warranty? If so, for how long? Does the warranty cover parts and service? Who is giving the warranty, the manufacturer and/or the dealer?

- Who pays for transporting the car back to the dealer if it breaks down?
5. Put all promises about the condition of the car, service to be provided, and financial terms in writing. Oral promises are usually not accepted in the event of a lawsuit.
6. Receive the certificate of title, copy of the bill of sale, and other appropriate documents.
7. Keep records of mechanical problems that arise after purchase. These include:
   - your own notes
   - receipts from repair shops or the dealer's mechanic
   - records showing the date and mileage on the car in addition to the problem experienced
   - schedule of trips you made to the dealer's repair shop
   - copies of signed work orders, canceled checks, and so on
8. Take immediate action to protect your rights. Contact the dealer if you are unsatisfied with your purchase. Follow up telephone calls with a letter to document your protest (see Figure 4.1). If the dealer refuses to cooperate, you can institute suit in small claims court (see Chapter 7) or a higher court. You should also contact your state's department of consumer affairs, the consumer fraud division of your state attorney general's office, and/or the Better Business Bureau (see Figure 4.2).

Private Individuals

The preceding strategies also apply to buying a car from a private individual. If you later pay for unexpected repairs, you may be able to recover the cost in small claims court (see Chapter 7). To do this, you will have to prove that:

1. The individual made inaccurate representations about the condition of the car. ("This car is in great shape; it was recently inspected and tuned up by a mechanic.")
2. You bought the car on the basis of these representations.
3. These representations were false, and the individual knew they were false at the time they were made.
4. You were damaged as a result.

When buying a used car directly from a private owner, ask these questions:

- What is the mileage?
- How has the car been driven? Highway travel or stop-and-go traffic?
- How long have you owned the car? Are you the original owner?
- What do you like best about the car?
- What major repair work has been done on the car? Has it been involved in any accidents? What happened to the car?
- Did you buy the car new? From whom? Does that dealer have service facilities?
- Why are you selling the car?
- Who is your mechanic/where has the car been regularly serviced? Are your complete service records available? May I inspect these records?
- Have you ever had any problems with rust? Has the car ever been painted? When?
- Are there any expenditures I must make to get the car in top condition? Can my mechanic inspect the car? (If the person says no, look elsewhere.)

For more tips on how to buy a used car, read *Consumer Reports Used Car Buying Guide.*

The Consumer Federation of America (which is composed of 240 non-profit consumer agencies) and the National Association of Consumer Agency Administrators (made up of 150 state and local government consumer protection agencies) report that car repair abuse is the *largest* source of consumer complaints, particularly now because people tend to keep their cars longer and older cars need more repairs.

Several states have accused a major company with franchise auto-repair shops throughout the United States of overcharging, recommending unneeded work, charging for work not done, and selling unneeded service using phony maintenance schedules. Other lawsuits have alleged improprieties as a result of charging fees to inspect a car just to find things to fix and allowing unqualified mechanics to diagnose problems, which causes more time (and expense) and the recommendation of more, unnecessary repairs.

> *One investigation conducted by California officials found the average repair resulted in an overcharge of $223. A New Jersey investigation accused 100 percent (all stores) of a major car repair franchise of recommending unneeded work!*

Avoiding Car Repair Abuses

Before taking your car to a new dealer or repair shop:

1. Talk to people who have patronized the firm and ask about the service they received. Call the BBB to discover if there are any complaints against the shop.
2. Describe what is wrong with your car completely and exactly, but don't tell the service manager or mechanic how to correct the problem. For example, if you brought your car in because the engine was running rough, don't announce that you need a tune-up. You may only need to have the timing adjusted, a much less expensive job.
3. Give the service manager or mechanic a written list of your car's problems, and keep a copy for yourself.
4. Do not automatically agree to everything the service manager or mechanic recommends. Ask for an explanation of any work recommended and why it is needed. Do not sign a blank work-order form.
5. Obtain a written estimate of all repairs and service. Get a second opinion before having expensive work done. Never authorize additional work over the telephone unless you trust the people you are dealing with.
6. Shop around at specialty service shops before taking your car to a dealership. Firms that specialize in certain kinds of work (muffler repair or brake jobs) may do the job at a lower cost.
7. Ask for the parts that are replaced. This can prove that work was actually done.
8. Examine your receipt. Question anything you don't understand. Save a copy of the receipt in case problems develop.

9. Try to patronize repair shops that employ mechanics certified by the National Institute for Automotive Service Excellence or are approved by the American Automobile Association. Look for shops that display an ASE sign and you'll improve the chances of using competent, experienced mechanics.

10. Newer car models now contain computers that control major car functions. Most newer models do *not* need tune-ups but rather replacement of defective parts. Avoid asking for a tune-up, since this may be unnecessary.

11. Inquire if the car's warranty will cover the problem so the problem can be corrected for free. Ask if the worker is paid a commission for all work performed; if so, get a second opinion.

12. Consider negotiating a reasonable flat fee for the job rather than being billed by the hour. This way, you may avoid inflated charges for high hourly rates and false billings for time not expended.

13. Be on the lookout for unnecessary maintenance and bait-and-switch ads. These get you to the shop for a low fee on advertised service, but once there, you are pressured into having other work done at great expense.

14. Always comparison shop before committing to major repair work.

15. Complain to the service manager or shop owner immediately if the work was not done properly. If you can't get satisfaction, send a letter by certified mail, return receipt requested, to document your claim, and consider filing a suit in small claims court.

Used-Car Lemon Laws

Many states have enacted used-car lemon laws, and other states have expanded new-car lemon laws to cover used cars. For instance, the New York statute requires that a warranty be offered on used vehicles sold by dealers for over $1,500, with refund or replacement available if the car cannot be repaired within three attempts or 15 days. The required warranty must provide free repair of major parts of the automobile (listed in the statute) and must have a duration of 60 days or 3,000 miles, whichever comes first, for cars with mileage of less than 36,000 miles, and 30 days or 1,000 miles for vehicles with over 36,000 miles. Failure to provide such a warranty is itself a violation, which may subject the dealer to punitive damages and attorney fees and costs incurred by the aggrieved consumer.

Check the law in your state to determine your rights by contacting your nearest BBB or department of consumer affairs. Notify the dealer, manufacturer, or company where the used car was purchased and request that repairs be promptly made by the seller. If after several attempts the condition is not alleviated, you can resort to the arbitration program in your state (if one is available) or initiate a private action to obtain a refund of the purchase price or a suitable replacement car. Follow the steps below to enhance your claim.

1. Write a letter to the manufacturer or dealer. State the model and vehicle identification number, the make of the car, and the date, purchase price, and place of purchase. Document the problem or defect. If possible, include a written statement from a mechanic or diagnostic center. In most states, you must notify the dealer and manufacturer of the defect within the warranty period, or one year of the date of delivery.
2. Schedule an appointment with the dealer to return the car. After the car is repaired, ask for a copy of the bill that shows what repairs were performed.
3. Save all documents and records. Prepare a diary of the steps you took to maintain the car in proper working condition (it was inspected on a regular basis) to show that the defect in the car was not caused by your negligence or abuse.
4. Take the car back to the dealer if the problem is not corrected. Speak to a lawyer or research the law in your state to determine the appropriate course of action to take if the defect persists.

JEWELRY, ART, AND ANTIQUE APPRAISALS, IMITATIONS

Jewelry, art, and antique appraisals are obtained to determine the proper amount of insurance needed to cover a purchase or loss, to determine the reasonable fair market value of an item donated to charity, and to compute appreciation of antiques and family heirlooms when distributing assets or figuring estate taxes. Appraisals are also commonly obtained for private sales and for determining the fair market value of marital property upon divorce.

Finding an Appraiser

Neither state nor federal law requires a personal property appraiser to acquire a license or certification. There are no formal standards of competence or minimum qualifications; anyone wishing to call himself or herself an appraiser may do so.

The American Society of Appraisers (ASA) requires its members to have degrees from accredited institutions, attend continuing education courses, adhere to ethical standards of the organization, have at least five years of accredited experience, and sit for a recertification exam every five years. The ASA maintains a directory of members and certified professional appraisers and their areas of expertise.

The Appraisers Association of America (AAA) is the second most valuable source for obtaining a qualified appraiser. Membership is acquired by a two-thirds vote of the seven-member board of directors. Certified members must pass a written and/or oral examination. The AAA has a similar, although less extensive, code of ethics as the ASA. Both groups can give you a list of reliable appraisers in your area. You can also contact your insurance company, bank, local university, museums, antique shops, or auction houses.

Choosing an Appraiser

Always choose an appraiser with a degree in the specialty that most closely relates to the object to be appraised. For example, estate appraisals are divided into such specialties as commercial, residential, and income properties, which are further divided into urban and rural properties. Other specialties include business valuations; machinery and equipment appraisals; technical valuations for boats, airplanes, and autos; personal property (divided into fine arts, antiques, furniture, jewelry, and household goods); and gems and jewelry. Avoid the dealer, jeweler,

Always choose an appraiser with a degree in the specialty that most closely relates to the object to be appraised.

curator, historian, interior decorator, artist, or auctioneer who appraises a variety of items.

When interviewing an appraiser, ask the following questions:

- How long have you been an appraiser?
- Is this your full-time profession?
- What is your general appraisal and education background?
- What specific experience do you have with the kind of property I wish to have appraised?
- Are you a member of a professional appraisal society? Which one(s)? Does that society teach, test, and certify?
- Have you undertaken any continuing education to keep you up-to-date in the field?
- What do you charge, and how do you determine your fee?
- For whom have you worked and what are your references? (Look for business references, banks, insurance companies, museums, etc., and confirm these references.)
- How do you arrive at your values? Do you have access to special libraries, relevant publications, current price indexes, and such?
- Will you document and support your opinion at a trial if necessary? Is there an extra fee for this? How much? (Think twice about hiring an appraiser who refuses to support an opinion.)
- May I see a sample appraisal report?

Tell the appraiser your specific needs, the item(s) to be appraised, and the purpose of the appraisal. Be sure your objectives are clarified so you receive a proper appraisal report.

Ethics

Appraisers must preserve the confidentiality of the subject matter, be objective, not charge excessive fees, and prepare clear, concise, and correct reports. It is unethical for an appraiser to accept an assignment and appraise an item in which he or she has an interest or contemplated interest in buying. Do not agree to a fee based on the value of the item; this may tempt the appraiser to overvalue an item to collect a higher fee.

Fees

Fees are usually determined by the type and purpose of the appraisal, the degree of difficulty, and the type of item appraised. Speak to several appraisers, and do not necessarily hire the one charging the lowest fee. Most good appraisers charge an hourly (from $35 to $150) or daily (from $350 to $1,500) fee. Expect to be charged for travel, research, and writing time. For large jobs, like an inventory of your home, appraisers often make a preliminary visit and, for a fee, give you an estimate of the entire cost. Try to get the appraiser to agree to deduct the estimate fee from the entire fee if you agree ultimately to hire him or her. Insist on a written contract or letter of agreement describing the arrangement (see Figures 4.3 and 4.4).

What Do You Get for Your Money?

The purpose of an appraisal is to establish rightful ownership of property, to identify the objects by describing their inherent characteristics, and to value the items based on the known comparable objects in the market-place. You should receive two copies of the appraisal, listing each item. A full description of each piece will tell you, to the best of the appraiser's ability, the age, characteristics, physical condition, and, if significant, national origin. When the maker—company, craftsman, or artist—is known, this will be included. Where pertinent, dimensions and silver weight will be stated. Numbers or sets will be included. Finally, each item or group will be assigned a value appropriate to the purpose of the appraisal—insurance, private sale, estate sale, donation for tax purposes, and so on. The date of the appraisal, purpose of the appraisal, and the appraiser's signature must be present.

Do not accept a scribbled, handwritten appraisal with misspellings, scant listings, and inaccurate numbers. An appraisal report that states "6 dining room chairs—$1,200" is meaningless.

What You Should Not Expect to Get for Your Money

Do not expect to have every single piece of property in your house cataloged, researched, and authenticated. For $500 to $1,000 you will receive an accurate, concise appraisal of the few special or most valuable items.

If You Are Exploited

You can file a written complaint with the American Society of Appraisers if the appraiser you hired is a member. This will commence a grievance procedure before the ethics committee, which determines if there has been a violation of their code of ethics. If a violation is found, the member may be warned, suspended, or expelled. The grievance procedure is a serious deterrent to would-be member violators.

You can also file a complaint with the local BBB or department of consumer affairs. In addition, you can seek redress in a court of law. Before an appraiser can be held liable for either negligent misrepresentation, intentional misrepresentation, or fraud, you must be able to establish that the representations made were (1) relied upon by you, (2) to your detriment, and (3) caused you harm—that is, monetary loss.

Gross negligence occurs when an appraisal is intentionally rendered false or made in reckless disregard for the true value of the object.

Finally, you can sue under the theory of breach of contract. If the services to be charged are in excess of $500 and/or the appraisal will take more than one year to complete, then you must have a written contract with the appraiser. If the services to be rendered are for a fee of less than $500 and will be performed in less than one year (as is usual), then your agreement may be oral. (However, smart consumers always get a written contract.)

In the case of an undervaluation, the monetary damage awarded is the difference between the fair market value and the purchase price of the item. In the case of overvaluation, damages are based on the difference between the purchase price and the fair market value (the salvage value or unauthentic value of the item). Sanctions of up to $1,000 can be imposed on the appraiser who knowingly overvalues a piece of property for charitable deduction purposes. If a corporation is involved, the penalty can be as high as $10,000.

Avoid Disclaimers

Watch out for appraisers who attempt to disclaim their reports by stating that they are not competent in scientific analysis, and thus are not responsible for incorrect appraisals, errors, or omissions due to failure to incorporate the scientific findings in the valuation.

An expert may try to obtain a covenant against liability in the appraisal contract. This clause is unethical—a professional owes a consumer the highest level of care. However, an appraiser may properly limit liability by stating that the valuation is for a particular purpose or person and/or is good for only a specific period of time.

Art Forgery

It is estimated that as much as 10 percent of all art sales involve a forgery of some kind. At the same time, risk of punishment or conviction for art forgery is comparatively small. A dealer can simply say that he or she was unaware that the object was a forgery at the time of the sale. Furthermore, forgery often can be proved only by expert opinion, and expert opinions are expensive, difficult to obtain, and frequently contradictory. In addition, since these experts are often art dealers, they are reluctant to risk losing customers.

> *The current popularity of prints has made them an attractive target for forgery. Jonathan was told that he bought an original print produced by an artist from a master plate of the artist's own design and approval and that it was a limited number personally signed by the artist. Unfortunately, Jonathan purchased a print reproduction that was produced from a photomechanical process (not requiring the supervision or knowledge of the artist). The forgery was so real that Jonathan paid a premium price for a "signed" reproduction that was not part of a limited edition.*

Methods

Forgery, the copying or alteration of a work of art for fraudulent purposes, is often classified according to the method of fabrication.

- Signatures are easily forged, either by adding the name of a famous artist to an unsigned work or by removing an existing signature and replacing it with that of a master.
- A forger can complete an unfinished work and sell it as an original masterpiece of the same time period.
- A forger can reproduce a specific masterpiece with the intent of selling the copy as the original work. Sculpture is easily forged by casting the original, thereby producing an exact replica. Prints can be forged easily when an artist fails to sign and number the work.

The buyer of antiquities must also exercise a degree of caution because the identification of ancient artists is often tenuous at best, and it is difficult to ascertain the chain of possession where an object is claimed to be freshly found. Similarly, the purchaser of ancient art should be suspicious in instances where a seller provides too detailed a description and representation regarding the origins of the object.

Methods of Detecting Art Forgery

There are essentially two methods of determining the authenticity of a work of art: connoisseurship and scientific analysis. A trained art connoisseur or art historian is well versed in the history of the period in which he or she is a specialist, and is experienced in handling original works of art.

Although the specific approach varies, an art historian will typically begin the process of authentication by comparing the piece in question with the accepted body of the artist's work. For instance, types of paper, paints, and materials may be significantly different. Details in the work such as wardrobe, jewelry, subject, hairstyle, architecture, or setting may postdate the supposed year of execution.

Then, various methods are used to determine the date of the materials used, the type of materials used, and the techniques implemented in producing the work. X rays and similar tests are employed to examine layers of pigment and undercoatings, which in turn reveal the stages of artistic production as well as later alterations. X rays, however, require expert analysis because although underpainting may be indicative of a forgery, it may also indicate restoration, an artist's dissatisfaction with his or her own work, or a desire to economize by reusing a discarded canvas.

Going, Going, Gone

When buying from dealers, shops, galleries, and shows, you have plenty of time to study an object and make up your mind. At an auction, there's less time for hesitation.

When attending an auction, particularly for the first time, it is a good idea not to make a bid until you learn the rules regarding how the auction is conducted. For example, how much of a deposit is requested after a purchase is made? Must the check be certified? What happens if you fail to pay the balance within the requested period of time—do you lose your deposit? These and many other conditions of conduct and sale should be spelled out in the contract between the customer and the auction house. Read it carefully before making a bid. The BBB suggests that abuses can be avoided by dealing only with reputable auction houses. Yet abuses occur in even the most reputable auction houses (i.e., one common scheme involves groups of people working for the house getting together to drive up the price of an object). Do not be drawn into paying more than you think an object is worth.

Attend the preview held before the sale. Purchase the catalog, then study the items on display and make notes in the catalog of their size, age, and condition. The catalog will give dollar estimates for, as well as descriptions of, the items for sale. Make a written list of what you really want and stick to it. Don't give in to auction fever. During the auction, write down what each item sells for and use the catalog as a guideline in the future.

Fine Jewelry

Guidelines established by the FTC in cooperation with the jewelry industry state that the word *gold,* used by itself, means all gold or 24 karat (24K) gold. Because 24K gold is soft, it is usually mixed with metals that will increase its hardness and durability.

The "karat" marking tells what proportion of gold is mixed with the other metals. If 14 parts of gold are mixed with 10 parts of base metal, the combination is 14 karat (14K) gold. The higher the karat rating, the higher the proportion of gold in the object. The lowest karat gold that can be marketed as gold in the United States is 10 karat. Jewelry does not have to be marked with its karat quality, but most of it is. If there is a karat quality mark, next to it must be the U.S. registered trademark of the person or company that will stand behind the mark, as required by the National Gold and Silver Stamping Act.

"Plated," "gold-filled" (GF), "gold overlay," and "rolled gold plate" (RGP) describe jewelry that has a layer of at least 10 karat gold mechanically bonded to a base metal. If such jewelry is marked with one of the terms listed above, the term must follow the karat quality of the gold used (e.g., "14K Gold Overlay").

Jewelry marked "silver" or "sterling silver" must contain 92.5 percent silver under jewelry industry guidelines. The mark "coin silver" is used for alloys containing 90 percent silver.

Gemstones

To qualify as "gemstones," minerals must possess beauty (affected by color, transparency, and brilliance), which is brought out by cutting; durability (the stone's hardness and toughness); and rarity (taking into consideration size and quality). Some organic materials—including pearl, coral, amber, and jet—are also used in jewelry.

Pearls

It takes years for an oyster to produce a fine, large pearl. The quality and value of pearls are determined by:

- lack of blemishes or spots
- roundness
- luster
- tint (Rose-tinted and silver pearls are the most valuable.)
- size (The larger the pearl, the greater the cost.)

A pearl necklace or any strung pearl item requires careful matching of size, roundness, luster, tint, and skin texture. Most pearls today are cultured; oysters are artificially stimulated to grow pearls. Basically, the same criteria for cultured and natural pearls determine value. But a pearl must be described as cultured or natural, and this should be stated on your bill of sale, since natural pearls are more costly than cultured pearls.

Some cultured pearls are dyed and made silver-blue or pinkish. Ask if the color is natural, and have the answer written in your receipt.

Synthetic (simulated or fake) pearls are sold everywhere, and good imitations have been mistaken for cultured pearls. Some people run the pearl gently between their teeth. The cultured or genuine pearl will have a mild abrasive feel; the imitation is often slippery smooth. When in doubt, seek the advice of a qualified gemologist.

Natural, Synthetic, and Imitation Stones

As their names indicate, natural stones are found in nature; synthetic stones are made in a laboratory. A synthetic or imitation stone cannot legally be offered for sale without disclosing that it is not natural. Similarly, a stone that does not have the same composition as the natural stone must be described as "imitation" or a similar word. In either case, you must be clearly informed if the stone is not natural.

Units of Measurement

Gemstones may be measured by weight, size, or both. The basic unit for weighing gemstones is the carat, which is equal to one-fifth of a gram. Carats are divided into 100 units, called "points." For example, a half-carat gemstone weighs .50 carats or 50 points. When gemstones are measured by size, this is expressed in millimeters. Pearls are expressed in millimeters because they usually are sold by diameter measurement.

Watches

If a watch costs $15 or more and comes with a written warranty, the law requires that the warranty be available to you prior to buying the product.

If you are considering an expensive watch, you may want to compare warranties as you compare prices.

Buying Fine Jewelry and Watches

Before buying any special piece of jewelry, ask the salesperson some key questions.

- If the item has a stone, is it natural, synthetic, or imitation?
- What enhancement methods, if any, have been used?
- If the gemstone has been enhanced, is the change permanent?
- What special care is needed?
- Will the seller write on the sales slip any information on which you relied in making the purchase, such as the gem's weight or size? Some jewelers also supply a grading report from a gemological laboratory.
- Is a warranty or guarantee provided on the watch?
- Which watch parts and repair problems are covered by the warranty? Which are excluded? For example, some warranties may not cover replacement of a watch crystal or case.
- Who pays shipping costs if the watch must be returned for repair— you or the company?
- How long does the warranty last?
- Where can you get the watch repaired under the warranty?
- What will the company do if a watch fails or a chain breaks and it. cannot be repaired? Will the company replace it or return your money?
- What are the conditions or limitations on the warranty? For example, some warranties may be limited to the first purchaser.

What to Do About Problems

Although the FTC won't intervene in individual disputes, it is still interested in hearing about problems that involve gold jewelry, gemstones, watches, or warranties. When sending complaints to the company, you can send copies of that correspondence to the Federal Trade Commission, Public Reference, Washington, D.C. 20580.

For information on fine jewelry or related subjects, write to the Jewelers Vigilance Committee, 1185 Avenue of the Americas, New York, N.Y. 10036.

ELECTRONIC EQUIPMENT SALES AND SERVICE MISREPRESENTATIONS

The rapid development of computer technology has caused problems for consumers. People who bought computers several years ago now find that their hardware has become outdated, is difficult and costly to maintain, and is not compatible with new software programs. Others, not familiar with computer technology, are misled by high-pressure salespeople who offer systems promising to do specific chores but that fail to deliver.

Avoiding Exploitation Before You Purchase

Before you buy a computer, know what the system is supposed to accomplish. Familiarize yourself with basic computer phraseology. Talk to friends and business associates to learn what they use. Prepare a list of points to consider before speaking with a salesperson. This should include:

- the software you wish to buy
- the cost of the hardware and any hidden service and installation charges
- the system's power, reliability, speed, memory capacity, and potential for expandability
- the system's ease of operation, programming, and memory
- the company's guarantees, warranty, and maintenance policies
- the tax ramifications of your purchase (a salesperson may be unable to explain this)

Comparison shop to get an idea of the kinds of systems and deals available. Be aware of the relative costs of each component. Sometimes a package deal will save you money; sometimes it won't. If you know absolutely nothing about computers and intend to make a sizable investment, consider hiring a consultant. Computer consultants act like real estate brokers. They shop around and help you select equipment to fill your needs. Ask for references and check them out. Be sure you know exactly what the services will cost.

Write down all promises made by a salesperson regarding how the system will perform, its capabilities, and what it will do. This may help you recover damages in the event of a future dispute.

Negotiating Points

Software. Decide what software you intend to use before you buy the hardware. The software tells the computer what to do; without it, the computer cannot do the job properly.

Some people hire computer programmers to write programs specifically suited to their needs (custom software). Others hire consultants to perform the programming. The majority of purchasers use existing programs (packaged software). Regardless of the type of software used, legal problems frequently develop.

Decide what software you intend to use before you buy the hardware. Then select a compatible hardware system.

- The software cannot be properly implemented into the system.
- The software fails to accomplish promised results.
- The software is misused by the purchaser.

Lawsuits often arise because the software fails to perform a specific job. This happens when the salesperson fails to describe clearly the specific functions the software can perform.

Consider the following points before selecting software:

1. *Function.* Define what the program will accomplish.
2. *Ownership.* Will the software be rented for one time, multiple, or unlimited use? Can it be purchased, or is it being made available on some other basis?
3. *Revisions.* If the seller updates the software on a regular basis, will you receive revised versions? Will you have to pay for this?

How long will you receive program revisions? If additional training is required, who pays for it?

4. *Implementation.* Can the software be used in another computer system, or are you restricted to using it in only one system? If no restrictions are imposed, be sure that additional fees will *not* be charged.

5. *Assistance.* Will the seller provide help if the program isn't working properly?

6. *Assurances.* Is the program "error-free," or are you purchasing it "as is"? If you are acquiring the program as is, demand a demonstration *before paying* to be sure that the program works to your satisfaction.

7. *Payment.* Is payment due on signing of the contract, when the software program is delivered, after it is installed, or after you receive a satisfactory demonstration? You may find a *progress payment schedule* advantageous (one-third of the amount on signing, one-third on installation, and the balance on satisfactory completion).

8. *Time restraints.* Do you need the software by a specified date? If so, the agreement should state that "time is of the essence." It should also say, if possible, that if you don't receive the functional software by a certain date, you can cancel the agreement, recover your deposit, and sue for damages. If you are to receive the software in stages, ask for periodic written reports. You can then make alternative plans if the seller cannot make timely delivery.

9. *Liability.* The contract should state that:
   - The seller is not violating copyright and other laws by selling you the program.
   - The seller will indemnify and hold you harmless.
   - The seller will pay for all costs of legal representation should you be sued by a third party through no fault of your own.

10. *Restrictions.* The seller will probably impose restrictions on your use. Most companies spend substantial sums of money to develop computer programs and do not permit purchasers to copy or disclose the contents or results to unauthorized third parties. Try to limit these restrictions. In any event, be sure they are not violated.

Hardware

Select a hardware system that is compatible with your software. Many computer manufacturers sell adaptable software programs, but you are not limited to selecting programs from the manufacturer. Try to buy a computer with:

- a large memory capacity
- sufficient power
- ability to be upgraded to handle more sophisticated software programs
- a proven track record, and not an experimental model

Payment. There are a number of ways to structure the deal. These include an outright purchase for cash; a purchase with financing from the seller, bank, or lending institution; a close-end lease; or a lease with an option to purchase.

Shipping instructions. Insist that the seller pay for preparation, shipping, and transit insurance. Try to take title only *after* the hardware has been delivered, assembled, and become functional.

Inspect the system immediately when you receive it to be sure that it wasn't damaged in transit. Request that it be assembled as soon as possible. This will increase your rights.

Delivery date. Include the date you expect the system to be delivered and installed. If time is of the essence, specify this in the contract. Time the delivery and installation of the hardware to the approximate date you expect to receive your software program. You may avoid paying for hardware that cannot be operated because essential software has not arrived.

Disclaimer clauses. Computer manufacturers often seek to limit their legal exposure in the event the computer fails to function properly. This is called a "disclaimer," or "limitation of liability" clause. The following is an example:

The manufacturer's entire liability and the customer's exclusive remedy shall be the adjustment, repair, or replacement of defective equipment. The manufacturer's liability for damages to the customer for any cause whatsoever, and regardless of the form of action, shall be limited to the greater of $5,000 or the purchase price stated within.

These clauses are unfair, and judges often refuse to enforce them against consumers.

Service contracts. If you want a service contract (most personal computer users do not need one), be sure you know exactly what you are getting. Some contracts cover parts only; others require you to bring in the system. There may be a hefty charge if the fault is your own operation or if your contract contains tricky "void" clauses.

How to Avoid Problems Before They Occur

1. Beware of sales misrepresentation: The sales talk is the time to get answers to your questions. Have a list of what you want to ask. Don't allow the salesperson to tell you what you need—you tell him or her.

    Don't buy on the basis of a fancy brochure. Demand to see a working prototype or program application before making an investment.

    Under the law, express warranties are created when a manufacturer (through its salespeople) makes statements of fact about the capabilities of a product or service. If you rely on these factual representations, purchase the product or service, and the statements prove to be false, you are entitled to recover damages. Writing down statements (about how the computer will perform in a certain situation) may help you prove your claims.

2. Beware of unusually low prices. Some companies offer a low price by stripping off standard components and then selling them back to you as costly accessories. Low prices might also indicate reconditioned equipment or cheap imitations. Always try to get a warranty, even when buying discounted merchandise.

3. Since software can contain a virus, be careful dealing with third parties. Ask if the disk has been tested for viruses before using it in your system.

4. Be particularly wary of buying used equipment. It may not be covered by a warranty or it may already be out of date, making it difficult to service.

5. Get a written contract: Before spending several thousand dollars, review the agreement carefully. Standard contracts are prepared by legal staffs of computer vendors and contain clauses that benefit the seller, not the buyer.

   Most computer hardware and software manufacturers and dealers refuse to negotiate standard sales and service agreements in the $1,000–$5,000 range. These contracts seldom vary from one dealer to the next, so consumers have trouble shopping for better terms and warranties. However, you or your lawyer can probably negotiate more favorable terms if a more expensive purchase is involved.

   Some sales contracts limit damages to the purchase price. While this clause can cut off your rights, don't assume you are precluded from recovering damages if you sign a standard contract with a disclaimer limiting your remedies. Although the law varies considerably from state to state, many judges find such clauses unconscionable, and therefore unenforceable. Always try to negotiate, but recognize your rights even if you sign a standard computer contract.

6. Be sure to fill out and return all registration cards. This allows the company to inform you of any problems with the product and how to correct them.

7. Don't pay the final installment until all flaws are corrected.

8. Keep accurate records after you acquire the equipment. Your contract, correspondence, and letters of protest will help prove your claim in the event of a dispute.

Refund and Delivery Rights When Purchasing Appliances, Furniture, and Large Electronic Items

In general, consumers are entitled to a refund for defective or damaged goods (not marked "as is") and misrepresented items. Most states have no typical refund law that applies to all retail establishments—refunds range from "100% money-back guarantees" to "no refunds or exchanges," depending on the retailer. But in some states, the law requires that refunds be given when policies are not properly posted. For example, retailers who do not give a cash refund within 20 days must conspicuously display their policy by attaching it to the item itself, at each cash register or point of sale, or making the policy clearly visible at each store entrance. The sign must tell whether the merchant gives refunds, and if so, under what conditions. You must also be told of time limits in which to obtain the refund and whether you are entitled to a cash refund or store credit. Check the law in your state by calling your local Better Business Bureau.

> *Cynthia purchased an expensive custom couch from a specialty home furnishings store. The salesperson assured her that the couch would be shipped to the store from North Carolina, where it was manufactured, in a few weeks. Cynthia wrote "time is of the essence" on the sales purchase agreement, with an outside delivery date of two months. Two months later, the salesperson called Cynthia to advise that the couch was still not there but "not to worry, it should be delivered in a few more weeks." Furious, Cynthia canceled the contract by certified letter, return receipt requested, and demanded the return of her deposit. She threatened in writing to contact the Better Business Bureau when her sizable deposit was not returned. Her deposit, with interest, was returned shortly thereafter.*

Under the laws of some states, businesses that sell home furnishings and major appliances are required to list the delivery date or range of dates in writing on your contract or sales slip at the time the order is taken. The business must deliver the merchandise by the latest stated delivery date unless you are notified of the delay and agree to the revised delivery date. If the company fails to deliver the goods by the original promised date and you do not consent to the delay, you can:

- cancel the contract and obtain a full refund of your deposit or partial or full payment within two weeks of the company's receipt of your request
- negotiate a new delivery date
- cancel the contract and obtain a credit for the deposit
- select new merchandise

If the delay was caused by a factor not in the retailer's control, such as a labor or shipping strike, or it was your fault, then the above does not generally apply.

If you do not receive goods on time, document your cancellation in writing, sent by certified mail, return receipt requested. The letter should state the amount of money to be refunded and when you expect to receive it. It should also state the name(s) of the persons spoken with and other pertinent facts.

Appliance Repair

Many appliance manufacturers have trained repairpeople who are skilled in a particular brand of appliance and will use parts specifically manufactured for that model and brand. You will save yourself a good deal of trouble if you call in the brand, model, and serial number from the nameplate when you make your initial call for help. (The nameplate is usually tucked away near an inside door.) Should you have continuing problems with your appliance and/or authorized repairs, you may try to resolve these by writing to:

> Major Appliance Consumer Action Panel
> 20 North Wacker Drive
> Chicago, Ill. 60606

MACAP is an industry-sponsored but independent group of consumer experts who receive and act on complaints from appliance owners.

Finally, think seriously before purchasing an extended warranty or a service contract for your appliance or electronic equipment. Service contracts are regularly "pushed" on consumers by store salespeople with good reason: Often the salespeople receive large commissions on them. *Consumer Reports* recommends that consumers think twice before wasting money on such contracts. When buying a new television, CD player, or other expensive equipment, chances are the device will not need to be repaired until long after the purchase and after even the "extended" warranty has expired.

FIGURE 4.1 Sample Letter to Used-Car Dealer

Your Name
Address
Date

(Name), President
ABC Used Car Sales
Anyplace, U.S.A.

Dear (Name):

On (date) I bought a used (describe make, model, year, service number, color) for the sum of $XXXX. At the time of the sale, you stated that the car was a "cream puff," in perfect mechanical condition.

It was agreed that your shop would perform any and all repairs if the car malfunctioned for any reason for a period of 60 days after the date of purchase. This was inserted into the sales contract and initialed by both of us.

Last week, while I was driving the car to (location), the car broke down. An AAA representative towed the car back to my home. Despite several telephone calls to you, the car is sitting in my driveway while you keep telling me "to be patient."

I require the use of an automobile for my business, and I am renting a replacement at the sum of $35 a day while your car is inoperative. Unless the car is repaired to my satisfaction immediately per our understanding, I will bring the matter to the attention of the Department of Consumer Affairs, the Consumer Fraud Division of the Attorney General's Office, and the Better Business Bureau, and I will consider instituting legal action against you.

Thank you for your cooperation in this matter.

Sincerely,
(Signature)

[Send certified mail, return receipt requested.]

FIGURE 4.2 Sample Letter to Department of Consumer Affairs

Your Name
Address
Date

Dept. of Consumer Affairs
Anyplace, U.S.A.

Re: Formal complaint against ABC Used Car Sales, license number XXX

To Whom It May Concern:

This letter is a formal complaint against ABC Used Car Sales.

On (date) I purchased a used car (describe make, model, year, serial number, color) from ABC Used Car Sales. A sales contract was signed that stated that ABC would perform satisfactory repairs at no extra charge for a period of 60 days from the date of the purchase.

On (date) the car broke down, and ABC refuses to repair it. This action has caused me significant damages, including (specify).

Please investigate the matter on my behalf. I am enclosing a copy of the sales contract, letter of protest sent to ABC, costs of renting a replacement car, and other documentation for your review.

Please contact me at the above address if you require any additional information or assistance.

Thank you for your prompt cooperation in this matter.

Sincerely,
(Signature)

cc: ABC Used Car Sales; Better Business Bureau; Attorney General's Office, Consumer Fraud Division.

[Send certified mail, return receipt requested.]

FIGURE 4.3 **Sample Appraisal Contract**

Name and Address of Client

In consideration of an appraiser's fee, (name of appraiser) hereby agrees to evaluate the tangible property belonging to (person items belong to) located at (place where items are located).

The approximate completion date will be _____.

I have agreed to pay your appraisal fee of $ _____ on receipt of the appraisal. This fee is based on your standard appraisal charges:

Signed at: _____ on this _____ day of 1993.

FIGURE 4.4 Sample Letter of Agreement with Appraiser

Your Address
Date

Appraiser's Name
Address

Dear (Name):

This letter sets forth the terms of my engagement of your services as an appraiser for the (describe item[s] to be appraised). This appraisal is sought for the purpose of (reason for obtaining the appraisal).

I agree to pay you $_____ as a retainer, which sum shall be applied against and deducted from the total fee due of $_____, which total sum shall be paid on presentment of a certified appraisal report (or set forth the terms of payment as discussed and agreed to with the appraiser).

You agree that the certified appraisal report that will be provided will accurately comply with all the requirements of the American Society of Appraisers. You further understand and agree that you will be responsible for all costs incurred by you in connection with your valuation of the (list the item to be appraised).

In the event of an inadequate appraisal, you further agree not to disclaim any and all liability. You agree to indemnify me and hold me harmless from any and all damages I may incur as a result of your false or inadequate appraisal.

If all of the above terms meet with your approval, please countersign both copies of this letter and return one to me. Thank you for your cooperation.

Very truly yours,
(Signature)

ACCEPTED AND AGREED:

_____

(name of appraiser)

5 Avoiding Mail, Telephone, and Door-to-Door Sales Fraud

MAIL FRAUD AND UNORDERED MERCHANDISE

The Mail-Order Merchandise Rule

The purpose of the Federal Trade Commission Mail-Order Merchandise Rule is to protect mail-order customers. According to this rule, companies that sell by mail or telephone must ship the order within 30 days of the time they receive the order. The only exceptions are if the company clearly states a longer period of delivery in its solicitation or if you do not send sufficient information (an incomplete address or payment).

If the company cannot ship your order within the advertised time, it must inform you in writing of the delay. It must also allow you to cancel if you do not agree to the delay. The company must then refund your money within seven days of receiving your request. If you paid by check or money order, your refund is a check. If you paid by credit card, you receive written notification of cancellation of the charge from your account. An advantage of paying by credit card is that your card issuer can withhold money if notified soon enough—that is, from 30 to 90 days, depending on the bank or credit company involved. The Mail-Order Merchandise Rule does not apply to COD purchases or serial delivery such as magazine subscriptions, although it does apply to the initial delivery.

If you do not respond to the notice of delay, the company has another 30 days to ship the merchandise. It may not delay shipment beyond the additional 30 days without your consent.

Unordered Merchandise

It is a violation of the Federal Trade Commission Act to send unordered merchandise through the mail unless it is a free sample marked as such or is sent by a charitable organization asking for, but not requiring, a contribution. Most states treat unordered merchandise as a gift. Persons sending unordered merchandise through the mail are prohibited from demanding payment, and you have the right to keep the goods or to dispose of the goods in any manner you wish. Moreover, billing for unordered merchandise may constitute mail fraud and/or misrepresentation.

Federal law also protects you if you accidentally order merchandise (you sign your name to accept receipt of samples of a product or you accept an unwanted package because of misleading language). You can return it without charge.

If you receive unordered merchandise that you find offensive or especially annoying, contact your local postmaster, the chief postal inspector in Washington, D.C., or the Federal Trade Commission in Washington, D.C. The FTC has nationwide jurisdiction over deceptive, unfair marketing practices. However, it does not usually get involved in individual disputes or "annoyance mail." The postal service is the appropriate agency to contact if the material you are receiving is explicitly sexual and sent to minors or if it is not so labeled.

In situations involving defective merchandise where there is a pattern of complaints about a company, the FTC can intercede to compel the return of all customers' money or fulfillment of their orders. It is also a good idea to contact your local Better Business Bureau to seek redress.

Substituted Merchandise

The same rules apply when receiving substituted merchandise: A seller may not send you substituted merchandise without your consent. And if you are not satisfied with your substitute merchandise, you are entitled to a refund. Mail-order merchants must issue refunds within 30 days of receiving your refund request and returned goods.

> *If you want to stop receiving unsolicited advertising mail, catalogs, and brochures, contact the Direct Mail Marketing Association, 6 East 43d Street, New York, N.Y. 10017. This organization can remove your name from the mailing lists of its members and stop delivery of most sweepstakes, contest offers, samples, coupons, and catalogs.*

Book and Record Clubs

Most book and record clubs operate on "negative options." You receive an announcement describing the next item to be shipped. The item is shipped automatically and you are billed for it unless you notify the company by a certain time that you do *not* want the merchandise. Under the FTC's rules, before shipping a selection the seller must send you an announcement identifying the selection and a form telling you the selection will be shipped unless you say no. The form must give either a date by which you must mail back the form or by which the form must be received by the seller. The seller must give you at least 10 days to mail back the form, and allow you to return, at its expense and for a full credit, any shipment you receive by mistake.

Never join a plan that fails to disclose clearly your rights under the FTC rule. Insist that the seller provide, and that you understand: complete

> *A magazine advertisement states it will provide consumers with original, hard-to-find recordings of many popular big bands and vocalists in tape, album, or CD form. Following the directions in the ad, Stacey sent a $19.95 money order. Three weeks later she received an album with barely audible outtakes. There is little Stacey can do because (1) no promise of quality was mentioned in the ad, (2) no money-back guarantee was offered, and (3) the company used a post-office box address that is no longer being used and cannot be traced to the principals of the operation.*

terms of the negative option plan and how to use it; any minimum purchase required to qualify as a member; the policy for postage and handling charges; the minimum number of items you must purchase to complete the plan; your right to cancel at any time; and how annual or periodic announcements will be sent to you and when. Finally, the same rules apply with respect to unordered merchandise as discussed above. If you terminate your membership but are then sent unordered merchandise, you may usually keep it at no cost.

Protecting Your Rights

1. Comparison shop. Find out if the merchandise is available from another mail-order source.
2. Check the advertising claims. Are they too good to be true? Check the description of the product and keep a copy of the ad or catalog from which you ordered.
3. Find out if there is a warranty. Does it offer your money back if you're not satisfied?
4. Check the time limit on delivery. Mail-order transactions must be shipped within the time stated in the company's printed or broadcast offer. If no time is stated, shipment must be within 30 days after the company receives the order, unless you agree to a delay.
5. Ask for a more detailed description of the product or its guarantee if you have doubts.
6. Make sure your name and address are clearly marked on the order form. If you are ordering a gift, be sure that the name and address of the person to whom you are sending it is legible.
7. Keep a copy of your order form and any letters you send to the company. Make sure you have the company's correct address.
8. Never send cash. Pay by check or money order. Be sure to include extra charges, shipping, handling, and sales tax.
9. Check the order immediately when you receive it. If it is expensive, check it before accepting delivery. If it is not what you ordered, do not accept it, and have it returned to sender. Notify the company in writing and keep a copy of your letter.
10. Contact your local postmaster or chief postal inspector if you have been victimized. The inspection service of the U.S. Postal

Service, headed by the chief postal inspector, is the law enforcement and audit arm of the postal service. This office performs security, law enforcement, and audit functions. It is responsible for investigating potential violations. Direct any grievance to their attention (see Figure 5.1).

> *For more information on mail orders, write to the Federal Trade Commission, Washington, D.C. 20580, for a free copy of "Shopping by Mail."*

COMMON SCAMS

Sweepstakes and Prizes

Telemarketing sweepstakes and promotions often use official-sounding names such as "Prize Redemption Center" or "National Claims Office."

Legitimate sweepstakes and prize awards never require you to purchase products in order to win.

Many include an 800 or 900 telephone number that you must call immediately in order to claim the prize. The catch is that you must buy the product in order to claim the prize. Or else the cost of the phone call far exceeds the value of the prize.

Legitimate sweepstakes and prize awards never require you to purchase products in order to win. If you have doubts about any offer, contact your local Better Business Bureau or state, county, or city department of consumer affairs. Find out if the FTC has any pending orders or cases against the company.

Through the National Association of Attorneys General (NAAG), state agencies operate a clearinghouse on telemarketing fraud to deal with interstate enforcement. You might want to contact them as well.

Mail-Order Ventures

Ads that claim you can get rich while working from your home are common, but most mail-order promoters do not have successful businesses. They are merely suppliers who seek to sell you advice and cheap products.

To avoid questionable mail-order promotions, the Better Business Bureau (BBB) recommends the following:

- Study the business and learn about its pitfalls as well as its opportunities.
- Evaluate the risks of establishing any business without experience.
- Investigate with the local BBB or chamber of commerce the reliability of anyone offering a sales proposition.
- Check the performance claims made for the products, and be sure they are supported by evidence.
- Demand proof of earnings, and verify the information with the people whose earnings are reported.
- Understand any contract or agreement before signing.

Telephone Sales and Other Telemarketing Scams

More than $10 billion is invested each year with swindlers and scam artists working the telephone. Pitches commonly include phony investment schemes, partnerships and tax shelters, bogus prizes, and commodities such as gold bullion. These scams typically promise unusually high rates of return.

Telemarketing Fraud

Two big telemarketing frauds involve vacation certificates and motorboat or motorcycle promotions. If you receive a vacation certificate, investigate whether airfare, hotel, and so on are included (usually they are not). Check to see what precautions the company has taken to protect you in the event of overbooking. Above all, do not attend any time-share presentation unless you are interested in what is for sale. If you are offered a motorcycle or motorboat at a reduced price, do not buy it. These products are inferior, and the premium and handling charges usually amount to more than they are worth.

Another common scheme involves people pretending they are IRS agents. Individuals are called and told they are entitled to a contest prize, insurance settlement, or money bequeathed by a distant relative—but first they must send the taxes on the prize to a post office box. Or people are informed that they are eligible for a low-interest loan provided they call an 800 or 900 number immediately. When you call, you discover you are charged an exorbitant fee for the call and that an expensive (say, $200) processing fee for the loan must be paid in advance. Operators pocket the loan-processing fees and disappear.

Scam artists follow up telephone calls to target consumers with visits to their homes or offices. Elderly people, widows, minorities, or owners of small businesses are often threatened with arrest if they don't pay tax arrears on the spot or provide their social security and credit card numbers. If this happens to you, always ask for the person to produce his/her photo ID card. Be skeptical regarding the nature of the visit. If you feel obligated to make a payment on the spot, never write a check to a purported IRS individual—make the check payable to the IRS directly. You can verify the address and identity of the IRS employee by calling 1-800-829-1040 or 1-800-366-4484 if you believe something is amiss.

To avoid telephone scams, remember the following:

- If the deal or proposal seems too good to be true, it probably is.
- Always get the name of the person, his or her address, and the name of the company. You may be able to find out if the investment is listed for sale by calling your state's consumer protection agency or attorney general's office.

If the deal or proposal seems too good to be true, it probably is.

- Never reveal your credit card number or accept unexpected telephone calls from strangers.
- Always ask for and review a written prospectus before investing. If a large amount of money is involved, retain the services of an attorney or accountant to review the written material and interview the telephone solicitor.

- If you must invest immediately or lose the opportunity, pass on the offer.
- Never invest money at any time or anywhere with someone you have not met.
- If you receive a call from a charity, don't automatically send money. Also be wary of offers made by sales companies that claim that a certain percentage of their sales go to charities. Investigate these companies and charities before making a donation.
- If you suspect you have been the victim of telemarketing fraud, contact your Better Business Bureau, Federal Trade Commission, state attorney general's office, U.S. postal inspector, or other appropriate agency.

The offices of some state attorneys general maintain a hot line for tele-fraud, and they network with the FTC to catch fraud across the country.

School Scams
(As published in *Consumer Reports,* May 1992)

Congress had a dream. In 1965, it established the Guaranteed Student Loan Program. The goal, said President Lyndon Johnson, was "to provide access to every student who wants to better himself through higher education."

The program encouraged lending institutions to offer students low-interest loans regardless of their economic status. The government told lenders it would subsidize the low-interest rates and pay off the loans if students defaulted. As a result, student loans, once unappealing to lenders, suddenly became a risk-free, money-making proposition.

Since 1965, the government has backed more than 50 million of these loans, worth more than $100 billion. The program has helped students pay their way through all types of educational institutions, from four-year colleges to trade schools.

But it has also lost more than $13 billion to defaults. In December 1989, a Senate subcommittee began a year-long investigation to determine how the student-loan dream became a taxpayer's nightmare. Its conclusion: While many students who could have paid their debts didn't, the loan program also spawned an array of fraudulent schools that prey on unwary youths.

> *A California man told the* Los Angeles Times *that he borrowed $5,500 to enroll in an auto-repair course he had seen advertised. The first day of class he discovered that the school had no garage, no tools, and no cars. In a classroom across town, recent immigrants were spending their loan dollars learning the fine points of English grammar by watching—over and over again—rented videos of Hollywood hits. Featured film:* La Bamba.

Finding a Good Vocational School

At last count, the United States had some 6,000 trade schools, offering training in 130 occupations, from auto mechanic to X-ray technician. How to tell good from bad?

First, rule out schools that don't have both a state license and accreditation from an independent agency approved by the U.S. Department of Education—imperfect screening, but screening nonetheless.

Tour the facilities. An up-and-up school should let prospective applicants talk freely with students and faculty members. Look for low student/teacher ratios and qualified instructors who have been there awhile.

Ask for documentation. How many students complete the training? How many get jobs in that field? In some states, licensing agencies require schools to submit that information annually. If so, the school should be willing to give prospective students a copy. Other important information to obtain in writing: the school's refund policy and a clear explanation of any student-loan obligations the student may incur. The U.S. Department of Education has a toll-free hot line (800-433-3243) through which students can learn a school's student-loan default rate. In general, the higher the rate, the riskier the school.

Contact the personnel offices of potential employers. Ask what training they require and what schools, if any, they recommend. Ask the school for a list of companies that have hired recent graduates.

Call the local Better Business Bureau. It may know whether the school has a problem past.

Finally—or first—check out other educational options. Community colleges may offer better training at more reasonable prices. Most require a high-school diploma or General Equivalency Diploma (GED) to enroll in professional courses; they often offer GED-preparation classes for a minimal fee. Education departments in some states can also supply lists of schools that offer free or low-cost training.

The technical school that the *Consumer Reports* staffer visited charges around $8,000 for 15 months of word-processor training. A few blocks away, she found a community college offering four-month courses in word processing for $875.

UTILIZING THE COOLING-OFF PERIOD

Door-to-door sales include everything from magazines and cosmetics to appliances and home improvement. High-pressure sales tactics can convince even the most savvy consumers to buy a product when seeing it in their own home. If you make a hasty decision that you later regret, both state and federal law allow you to cool off.

At the time of sale, the seller must give you notice of your cancellation right. This notice is in writing in your contract or on your receipt. Federal law also requires oral notice. In order to cancel, sign your name and the date of cancellation on the form and make a copy for your records. Mail before midnight of the third business day to the seller's address, and send by certified mail, return receipt requested. Upon receipt the seller must furnish you with a refund, including postage and shipping in most cases, or full credit within 10 business days. There are also provisions for returning the goods if they are in your possession.

In addition, if your state has a cooling-off law, your period of cancellation may begin once the seller provides you with a notice of cancellation form, which includes the name and address of the seller and a place to sign your name to effect cancellation. If the seller does not provide this form expeditiously, you can cancel by notifying the seller in any manner. Contact your local BBB for your state's law.

If no refund policy is specifically stated in the contract, you have 20 days after receipt of the merchandise to demand a cash refund or full credit if the merchandise is in "substantially good condition." You get the refund within 10 days after returning the merchandise.

Most cooling-off laws apply to sales that exceed $25. A seller cannot bypass this law by using separate receipts of under $25 for each item. The law protects private parties in the home, hotel and restaurant solicitations, or sales on street corners. It does not include mail or telemarketing sales; purchases of securities, insurance, or real estate; or emergency home repair. In the latter situation, you bear the loss in the event the services were not needed. This is to ensure speedy assistance in an emergency.

FIGURE 5.1 Letter Regarding Mail-Order Fraud

Your Name
Your Address
Date

Local Postmaster
Anyplace, U.S.A.

Dear Postmaster:

I believe I have been the victim of an illegal mail fraud.

On (date) I responded to an advertisement in _____. The ad stated that I would obtain (name or product), provided I sent $29.95 to (address of company).

Over two months have passed since I sent my check, and I have not received my purchase. In addition, I sent the company a letter on (date) to document my protest, and I have not received a reply.

Please investigate this matter on my behalf. I can be reached at the above address if you require additional information.

Thank you for your cooperation in this matter.

Sincerely,
(Signature)

Enclosures: copy of ad, canceled check, letter of protest

[Send certified mail, return receipt requested.]

---

6 Obtaining the Services You Pay For

CHOOSING A DOCTOR AND PROTECTING YOUR RIGHTS AS A PATIENT

When choosing a doctor, it is best to find one who is board certified or board eligible. To become board certified, a doctor must complete three to seven years of full-time training (an accredited residency) in the specialty and pass an examination offered by that specialty board. Some boards also require that a doctor practice full-time in the specialty before the examination. To determine if your doctor is board certified, call your state department of licensing or the American Board of Specialties (1-800-776-CERT). You can also refer to the *ABMS Compendium of Certified Medical Specialists,* available at the library.

It is also a good idea to select a doctor who is affiliated with an academic medical center where doctors are trained. This affiliation usually means that the doctor has teaching responsibilities and keeps up-to-date on new developments in the field.

If you believe you have been victimized by an incompetent doctor or have complaints regarding professional misconduct (sexual abuse, gross incompetence, alcoholism), you can sue the physician for malpractice in a private lawsuit or file a written complaint with your state department of health, which typically maintains an office of professional medical conduct. If your complaint is viable, it will be investigated (the process may take months). An investigation committee will decide whether the case should be given a hearing or referred to the appropriate peer group or local medical society. After a thorough investigation, the board may make recommendations for disciplinary action, including a formal reprimand, suspension from practice, or revocation of the doctor's license (rare).

Consultation

Before choosing a primary care doctor, ask for a consultation (most charge for this) and get answers to the following questions:

- How does the doctor handle emergencies when a patient needs to reach him or her?
- Who covers for the doctor at night and on weekends?

If the consultation is with a surgeon, try to find out the following:

- How many of these operations has the doctor performed? (Experts suggest that surgeons should perform an operation at least 100 times a year to stay expert and current.)
- What is the success rate for the procedure?
- What is the doctor's success rate for the procedure?
- If a new procedure is being recommended, what are the advantages and disadvantages versus the older procedure? What are the risks and the likelihood of benefit with the procedure?
- What will happen if you do nothing? Do you need the procedure immediately? Will the nature of the problem become clearer if you wait? Can the discomfort or the symptoms be controlled if you decide not to go ahead with the proposed treatment?

Before you undergo an expensive or possibly dangerous test, it is often helpful to ask:

- Will the result of this test pin down the diagnosis or let you know what to expect in the future?
- Will the result of this test change the decision to treat, or alter the type of treatment?

In addition, when medication is being prescribed, ask the following kinds of questions before beginning treatment:

- How effective is the drug?
- What are the risks or side effects?
- Do you have choices in the way the drug is administered?
- Can you use a generic alternative?
- Do you take the drug on an empty stomach or with food?
- Do you have to take the medication at any special time?
- Does the medication interact with any of your other medications or with any food or alcohol?
- How long will you need to take the medication?

Ask About Fees

- Are fees usually paid by insurance, or do they exceed "usual and customary" in this area?
- Will the insurance company be billed first, or must payment be received up front and the patient reimbursed later?

Hospitals and Emergency Rooms

Do not expect to be treated immediately in an emergency room unless you are suffering from a serious condition such as a heart attack, bleeding profusely, having a seizure, or giving birth. Average waiting time is one to six hours, depending on the seriousness of your problem and how busy the hospital is. Your right to treatment continues until discharge or until you are transferred to another hospital.

Whether you are suffering from a serious injury or minor fracture, you are entitled to an initial screening. This is usually conducted by a clerk or nurse. Once you fall within the category of "emergency" (which is generally what an average person would consider an emergency), you are entitled to be examined by a doctor.

Under federal law:

- A hospital must provide all patients with a medical screening examination to determine if an emergency medical condition exists.

- A hospital must provide stabilizing treatment to any individual with an emergency medical condition or woman in active labor prior to transfer.
- If the hospital cannot stabilize the patient, the patient may be transferred to another hospital if
  - •• the responsible physician certifies in writing that the benefit of the transfer outweighs the risk
  - •• the receiving hospital has space and personnel to treat the patient and has agreed to accept the patient
  - •• the transferring hospital sends medical records with the patient, and
  - •• the transfer is made in appropriate transportation equipment with life support if necessary

Your rights as a patient begin when you enter a hospital emergency room, doctor's office, or health maintenance organization (HMO). Be sure to clear your emergency treatment by telephone with your HMO or other insurer if you are insured under a plan that requires treatment at a particular institution or by certain designated doctors.

If a hospital knowingly and willfully, or negligently, violates any of these provisions, it can be terminated or suspended from the Medicare program. It could also be held liable for failure to take action against the attending physician. You can institute a malpractice action against a hospital in the event of a violation.

A hospital may not refuse to treat you in an emergency if you cannot pay, nor may treatment be refused on the basis of race, ethnicity, or religion. AIDS patients may not be refused available treatment.

In addition, the Joint Commission on Accreditation of Hospitals and the American Medical Association publish a Patient's Bill of Rights. This deals primarily with rights to privacy, respect and integrity, information, proper communication, and the right to refuse treatment or continuing care. This bill of rights can be used as evidence in a court to show that the hospital and/or its staff deviated from a standard of care it has adopted as house policy or from custom generally recognized throughout the hospital community. California, Illinois, Kentucky, Maryland, Massachusetts, Michigan, Minnesota, New York, Rhode Island, and Vermont have enacted statutes or regulations to the same effect.

> *In one case a private hospital admitted an eight-year-old boy suffering from a bone infection. The bill for treatment was $3,000, but the boy's father could pay only $787. The hospital discharged the boy for failure to pay his bills and instructed the father that the boy would be safe at home under the care of a physician. In fact, the physician was not able to provide proper care at home, and the boy's condition worsened. At the trial, the court found the hospital liable for negligent and wrongful discharge.*

If you do not go through the emergency room, you will be subject to the admission procedure. If your personal physician is not arranging for your admission and discharge, there can be problems. There is no universal right to admission in a nonemergency situation. Although a hospital may not discriminate, house policy may disallow entry. Most hospitals either receive financial assistance under the Hill-Burton Act, which obligates hospitals to admit a certain number of indigent patients, or have adopted Medicaid (programs for the poor or disadvantaged) or Medicare (for those over 65). These hospitals cannot disallow entry on the basis of inability to pay, nor may Medicaid/Medicare participants be required to pay a deposit before admittance. Private hospitals can, however, deny admittance until a deposit is made. (If you are illegally denied admission, contact the HCFA.)

Admission is any act of a hospital employee on behalf of the patient, such as initially contacting a doctor for consultation or putting a patient in a hospital gown. You can be considered admitted even if you have not filled out forms including payment terms, insurance, consent forms, and possibly living wills. But if the hospital requests you to sign the forms and you refuse, it can deny admission.

Once you are admitted, a hospital may not detain you against your will unless it has proven you are mentally ill by testimony of usually two qualified psychiatrists (you will hurt yourself or others) or you are quarantined under the state public health law. If you are detained against your will for any reason, including inability to pay, this constitutes false imprisonment. (You have a cause of action against the hospital and/or staff regardless of physical injury.) Mental injury is presumed in such lawsuits.

Informed Consent

You have the right to informed consent, which consists of the following:

1. a description of the recommended treatment procedure
2. a description of the risks and benefits of the procedure, with emphasis on risks of death or serious disability
3. a description of the alternatives, including other treatments or procedures, together with their risks and benefits
4. the likely results of no treatment
5. the probability of success, and what the physician means by success
6. the major problems anticipated in recuperation, and the time it will take before you can resume normal activities
7. any other information generally provided to patients in this situation (This includes the identity of physicians involved in your care, use of removed organs, or how you can cross out all portions of the consent form that you do not agree to. You must also be informed if you are getting an invasive diagnostic test— such as a bone marrow aspiration or biopsy—or awaiting major surgery. This consent must be communicated clearly in a language you can understand.)

For routine treatment, consent can be implied from your behavior (such as waiting in line for an injection). But consent must be voluntary. If you are threatened or drugged, there has been no consent. If you are incompetent (you cannot understand the consent) or have been declared incompetent by a court of law, consent is obtainable from family members or from an appointed guardian in the event the family is acting contrary to your best interest. You can use or bring a living will, in which you designate a person to make treatment decisions for you in the event you are incapacitated (see Figure 6.1).

The doctrine of informed consent does not apply in an emergency situation if the risks are common and known to the average person, if you don't want to be informed, or if the doctor objectively believes that such information would be adverse to your interest.

There is a difference between a blanket consent form (usually signed at admission and allowing routine treatment) and informed consent (when there is the possibility of death or unknown injury subsequent to treatment). In general, blanket consent forms state "I, the undersigned, hereby grant permission for the administration of any anesthetic to and for the performance of any operation upon myself as may be deemed advisable by the surgeons in attendance at . . ." The more vague these forms are, the better chance of having a court set them aside.

> *Even though the necessity of ensuring informed consent is important in crisis-oriented situations, it is even more critical in elective procedures, especially when there is a possibility that the treatment might worsen a person's condition. In one case, a patient had skin blotches on his face. The doctor sanded a layer of skin off the patient's face, but this procedure made the blotches more noticeable. At the trial there was evidence that the doctor never mentioned the possibility of failure and that the probability of success with this procedure was only 40 percent. The court ruled in favor of the patient. It stated that since this procedure was elective (a nonemergency), the doctor was obligated to disclose all material facts that his patient would need to render an informed and intelligent decision.*

You can sue for malpractice in the case of injury due to an undisclosed material risk or an undisclosed safer alternative. Some informed consent forms contain provisions that attempt to waive the right to sue a doctor and/or a hospital for malpractice. A typical release or waiver reads: "The hospital is a nonprofit, charitable institution. In consideration of the hospital and allied services to be rendered and the rate charged therefor, the patient or his legal representatives agrees to and hereby releases the . . . hospital from any and all liability for the negligent or wrongful acts or omissions of its employees, if the hospital used care in selecting its employees." Such waivers, however, are probably not binding.

Consent can be withdrawn orally as long as you are conscious. In this case, destroy the old written consent immediately.

If you are a competent adult, you can refuse treatment. Proper refusal obligates your doctor and/or hospital to abide by it. However, you will have to sign a release, holding the doctor and/or hospital harmless for any results of stopping treatment.

According to standard surgical procedure, a doctor can engage in further surgery in the event of an emergency (discovery of acute appendicitis while treating a tubal pregnancy) or can extend the surgery within the general area of consent if there are no additional complications, such as repairing a double hernia when the diagnosis was a single hernia. However, if you specifically forbid further surgery, this is malpractice and/or battery. Malpractice statutes give you a longer time to sue (usually two and a half years) than battery action (usually one year).

You can also limit your consent to surgery by a particular physician or request to have a particular second physician present. If these wishes are not adhered to, this is also malpractice or battery.

Review the following points before you sign a consent form:

- You know the name and nature of your injury, illness, or disability, and the dangers or disadvantages of no treatment.
- You know the nature of the procedure recommended and the risks and benefits.
- You know whether there are other ways of treating the problem and know the risks and benefits of these other procedures. You believe that the procedure proposed is the best for you.
- You know the probability of success.
- You understand all that you have been told and can explain the procedure in your own words.
- Your doctor has answered all questions openly and has offered to discuss any additional concerns.
- You understand the meaning of all the words in the consent form.
- You agree to everything in the form. Your doctor is aware of any changes you made in the form.
- You know the identity and qualifications of the person or persons who will be performing this procedure.
- You have a clear head and an alert mind and are not too anxious or harassed to make a decision.
- You know you do not have to consent to this procedure.

Privacy

Your physician or health-care provider may not disclose any information about you to a third person not involved with your care and treatment, excluding the following:

- birth and death certificates (if a crime is suspected)
- contagious diseases must be reported, including AIDS but not infection with the HIV virus
- child abuse
- injuries inflicted by guns, knives, or other objects
- medical records and testimony routinely used in personal injury or malpractice cases
- use of records by agencies for survey purposes, accreditation, detection of fraud, and licensing
- if a patient threatens the life of another person and the doctor has a reasonable belief that the patient will carry out this threat

Confidential information may be optionally disclosed through implied consent (to nurses, doctors, and interns involved with your care) or by signing a general release (as opposed to a teaching hospital where disclosure is routine, assuming proper steps are taken to protect patient identity) that allows disclosure to insurance companies or welfare departments. Such a release can be set aside if too vague, and you can sue for invasion of privacy if the receiver used this information for other than the stated purpose.

You also have the following rights of personal privacy:

- You can refuse to see any or all visitors.
- You can refuse to see anyone not officially connected with the hospital.
- You can refuse to see persons officially connected with the hospital who are not directly involved in your care and treatment, including social workers and chaplains.
- You can wear your own bedclothes, so long as they do not interfere with treatment.
- You can wear religious medals.
- You can have a person of your own sex present during a physical examination by a medical professional of the opposite sex.

- You cannot remain disrobed any longer than is necessary to accomplish a medical procedure.
- Your case may not be discussed openly in the hospital.
- Your medical records may be read only by those directly involved in treatment or monitoring its quality.
- You can insist on being transferred to another room if your roommate is disruptive.
- As a patient in a teaching hospital, you can refuse to be a research subject.

Pregnant women have additional rights:

- •• You can have a female present during obstetrical or gynecological examinations. If this request is denied in a hospital, complain directly to the chief of the doctor's service. (If this request is denied in an office, contact your state licensing society and local medical society.)
- •• You can refuse to allow medical students or interns to examine you. If such examination occurs after protest, the hospital, doctor, and student/interns have committed battery and/or malpractice.
- •• You have the right to genetic counseling and screening, including but not limited to amniocentesis and ultrasound.
- •• You can refuse medical treatment and/or drugs (for example, caesarean, HIV screening, anesthesia, fetal monitoring).

There are specific rights for terminally ill patients:

- You have the right to know of the prognosis, unless you have waived this right and passed it on to a relative.
- You have the right to confidentiality (you can demand that your family not be told).
- You have the right to informed consent for any continuing treatment.
- You have the right to refuse extreme or life-sustaining treatment, including artificial nutrition and hydration. The best way to protect your rights in the event you become incapacitated is to create a living will, which simply states what treatment you want and do

not want. Several matters should be addressed in a living will, including the right to refuse intravenous fluids, antibiotics, or resuscitation. You might also want to give power of attorney to someone you trust (see Figure 6.2).
- You have the right to all the pain medication you need, including narcotics.
- You have the right to die at home.

Discharge

Assuming you are a competent adult, you can decide to leave the hospital at any time. Failure to sign a release form is not grounds to detain you. There is no obligation to sign a "discharge against medical advice" form.

Hospitals that participate in Medicare programs follow DRGs (Diagnosis Related Groups) in which the state pays a fixed rate per patient for a certain amount of days depending on the diagnosis. This is an average stay. If you need more care, the hospital may not force you to leave.

Hospitals are required to establish utilization review committees, which decide if an admission was unnecessary (within two days after entry) and whether discharge is appropriate. Your physician is given notice, with an opportunity to argue the decision. (An important effect of this is to determine if federal monies will be denied a patient.) The decision of the committee can be reviewed by the local social security office or by the U.S. Department of Health and Human Services if requested by you or your doctor. In any case, you and your doctor decide if discharge is in your best interest.

Your discharge is effected by written order of your doctor. If you feel that your discharge is premature, discuss it with your physician. If this is to no avail, you have the right to a consultation with another physician. If both doctors agree that you are well and you still refuse to leave, the hospital can physically remove you as a trespasser. However, they may use only reasonable force to do so. Insist on having the instructions in writing, and keep a copy handy for referral as needed until your condition has cleared up.

Upon discharge you are entitled to be informed about follow-up care. The failure to provide such instruction is a breach of care by the hospital and may be grounds for liability in the event injury results. Most hospitals provide forms for instruction, and some have social workers to explain self-care and to facilitate arrangements for long-term care if necessary.

HIRING A LAWYER AND ESTABLISHING FEES

Few legal problems disappear at a lawyer's touch, and lawyers cannot significantly reduce the time you must wait before receiving your day in court.

What a lawyer can and should do is zealously protect your interests. He or she should represent you competently, keep you informed, and bill reasonably for services. The good lawyer fights for you and protects you.

Lawyer-client disputes sometimes arise because:

- Fee arrangements are not spelled out.
- Clients are not consulted regarding settlement negotiations.
- Phone calls are not promptly returned.
- Work on legal matters is put off.
- Potential conflicts of interest are not fully disclosed.
- Client funds are used improperly.

Determining When You Need a Lawyer

Laws are complicated, and people need lawyers to guide them properly. We are exposed to hundreds of different commercial transactions (buying a house, signing contracts, divorce, etc.) that require legal services. In addition, lawyers advise us about taxes and labor regulations, social security, and administrative and other legislative enactments. Some people experience financial difficulties or run afoul of the law. Others require estate planning, including the preparation of wills. Thus, the services of a lawyer are often required.

Finding a Lawyer

The best way to determine if you have a problem requiring legal attention is to speak to a lawyer. He or she should be selected with care. A lawyer who competently represents clients in contract law may not be qualified to represent the same client in a personal injury lawsuit.

- Call your own lawyer, if you have one, and ask what he or she thinks about your problem and whether a meeting should be scheduled.
- If you have never dealt with a lawyer, ask friends, relatives, or business associates if they can recommend someone.
- Call your local bar association and ask for the names of lawyers who specialize in your particular problem. Some of these associations maintain lists of lawyers who do not charge more than $25 for the first half-hour of consultation (some lawyers will give you a free 30-minute consultation). Both prominent and neophyte lawyers list their names with the bar association. If experience is important, be sure to say so.

Be careful not to automatically choose a lawyer solely on the basis of his or her advertising. Claims about fees, expertise, and success rates can be misleading. Also, don't seek recommendations from bail bondsmen or hospital personnel: They may not be objective.

The Initial Interview

The initial interview serves several important purposes: It helps you obtain a sound evaluation about your legal problem, and it helps you decide if you should hire this lawyer. The initial interview is also the time to discuss important working details, such as the fee arrangement.

Bring all pertinent written information with you, such as copies of employment contracts, checks, letters, bills of sale, photographs. Tell the lawyer everything related to the matter. Try to communicate relevant information without inhibition—your discussion is confidential. All of this will facilitate the lawyer's work and time.

Once the lawyer has the facts and a lawsuit is considered, he or she will:

- decide whether your case has a fair probability of success after considering the law in the state where the suit will be brought
- give you some estimate as to how long the lawsuit will last
- estimate the legal fees and disbursements
- tell you what legal papers will be filed, when, and what their purposes are

- discuss the defenses your opponent will probably raise and how you will deal with them.

If the lawyer sees weaknesses in your case or believes that litigation will be unduly expensive, he or she may advise you not to sue.

One of the best ways to protect yourself is to request an opinion letter. Opinion letters spell out the pros and cons of a matter and help you evaluate whether you should proceed and spend money to accomplish your objectives. Even though you will probably be charged for the time it takes to draft the letter, it is usually worth the fee.

Should You Hire the Lawyer You Have Met?

It is important to feel that the lawyer is open and responsive to your needs, that he or she is genuinely interested in helping you, that he or she will answer your inquiries promptly, and that your case will be prepared and handled properly. Although it is difficult to predict how well the lawyer will perform, there are certain clues to look for at the interview.

- Are you received on time?
- Does the lawyer leave the room frequently during the interview, or permit telephone calls to intrude?
- Does he or she demonstrate boredom or lack of interest by yawning or finger-tapping?
- Is he or she a clock watcher?
- Does he or she discuss the fee arrangement with you up front?

Other Items to Clarify at the Interview

- What is this lawyer's reputation? Ask if you can talk to a previous client. Don't be impressed by the law school he or she attended— most do not give their graduates practical experience. In fact, many less-prestigious schools offer superior nuts-and-bolts training.
- Be sure that the lawyer you interview will be the one working on your case. People often go to prestigious firms expecting their problem to be handled by a partner. They pay large fees but wind up being represented by a junior associate.

- Will the lawyer be available? Ask what his or her normal office hours are. Request that he or she return phone calls within 24 hours, or that a secretary or associate return your phone calls if the lawyer will be unavailable for an extended period. In return, make it clear that you will not call unnecessarily.
- Will the lawyer work on your matter immediately? The legal system is often a slow process and there are statutes of limitations. Insist that the lawyer begin working on your case as quickly as possible.
- Are there conflicts of interest? One of the rules of professional ethics, which lawyers are bound to follow, states that a lawyer should avoid even the appearance of impropriety. Always ask the lawyer up front if he or she perceives any potential conflict of interest.
- How will your funds be handled? Lawyers are obligated to keep client funds in separate accounts. This includes unearned retainer fees. The rules of professional conduct state that a lawyer cannot "commingle" client funds with his or her own. A lawyer must notify you immediately when funds are received on your behalf. You must also receive an *accurate account* of these funds—a complete explanation of the amount of money held by the lawyer, its origin, and the reason for any deductions. Tell the lawyer to place your funds in an *interest-bearing escrow account.* Later on, when your funds are remitted, be sure that the interest is included in the amount returned to you.

The major factor in determining whether you should hire a lawyer is the amount of experience and expertise he or she has handling legal problems similar to yours. Use a lawyer who devotes at least 30 percent of his or her practice to your area.

Fees

Many lawyers charge a nominal fee, if any, for a first meeting; after that, fees should be charged only for actual time spent working on the matter. Charges are based on the amount of time and work involved, the difficulty of the problem, the dollar amount of the case, the result, the urgency of the problem (a real estate closing the lawyer must handle the next day should command a higher fee than the same closing that takes place in a month), and the lawyer's expertise and reputation.

Costs are expenses that the lawyer incurs while preparing your case or working on your matter. These include photocopying, telephone, mailing expenses, and court filing fees. Be certain you know which of these costs you must pay. Frequently, a lawyer cannot tell you exactly how much his or her services will cost because he or she is unable to determine the amount of work that is involved. Ask for an estimate. If the figure seems high, consider speaking to another lawyer.

Flat fee. In a flat fee arrangement, you pay the lawyer a specified sum to get the job done. Preparation of a simple will, handling of an uncontested divorce, the forming of a small corporation, adoption, and certain commercial contracts are often performed for a flat fee.

Flat fee plus time. Here, a sum for a specified number of hours is charged. Once the lawyer works more hours than are specified, you are charged on an hourly basis (see Figure 6.2).

Hourly rate. Most lawyers bill on an hourly basis. This can range from $75 to $300 or more an hour.

Contingency fee. Here the lawyer keeps a specified percentage of any money recovered via a lawsuit or settlement. Contingency fee arrangements are common in personal injury and medical malpractice lawsuits. Many people favor contingency fee arrangements because they are not required to pay legal fees if their case is unsuccessful.

Some types of contingency fees are not permitted. For example, a lawyer cannot structure the size of his or her fee on the type of verdict obtained for a client in a criminal matter. Contingency fees are also looked upon unfavorably in matrimonial actions (because they are viewed as encouraging divorce). Nor are contingency fees that exceed maximum allowable percentages (typically 40 percent) allowed in personal injury suits.

There are distinct advantages and disadvantages to each fee arrangement. When you pay a flat fee, you know how much you will be charged, but you do not know how much care and attention will be spent on your matter. The hourly rate might be cheaper than a flat fee for routine work, but a lawyer can "pad" timesheets to increase the fee. In addition, although contingency fee arrangements are beneficial if your case will be very expensive to try, the arrangement can encourage a lawyer to settle for less money rather than go to court (see Figure 6.3).

Insist that your fee arrangement be spelled out in writing and that all provisions be clearly explained. The lawyer may ask for a retainer at the interview. This guarantees the availability of the lawyer to represent you and is an advance paid to demonstrate your desire to resolve your problem via legal recourse.

Ask whether the retainer is to become part of the entire fee and whether any unused part is refundable. Be sure that interest will not be imputed if you are late paying fees. Request that all fees be billed periodically and that billing statements be supported by time records that include the number of hours (or partial hours) worked, the people contacted, and the services rendered. Some lawyers may be reluctant to do this, but by receiving these documents and statements on a regular basis, you will be able to question inconsistencies and errors before they get out of hand. You will also be aware of the amount of the bill as it accrues, and can pay for it over time if you choose (see Figure 6.4).

Should You Settle a Case?

Civil actions usually take up to five years. By accepting a fair settlement early on, you have use of the money, and the proceeds can be invested to earn more money. You eliminate large legal fees, court costs, and the possibility of eventually losing the case at trial.

However, if you have a good case, you may get a larger settlement by waiting before accepting a settlement. This is especially true in personal injury lawsuits. Most trial lawyers believe that larger settlements are obtained by waiting until a case reaches the courthouse steps. The reason seems to be that insurance companies do not negotiate in earnest until the moment before a case is tried. Time is on the side of the insurance company. It makes money by holding settlement funds and investing them.

The decision to accept a settlement should be made jointly with your lawyer. He or she knows the merits, pitfalls, and true value of the case better than you. However, do not be pressured into accepting a smaller settlement than you think you deserve.

Instruct your lawyer to provide you with a detailed explanation of the pros and cons of settling your case. Inform him or her that you prefer to control your affairs, including the decision of settling your claim. Your lawyer cannot settle or compromise the case without your approval. If he or she does, you can sue for malpractice.

Should You Change Your Lawyer?

You have the right to change lawyers at any time if there is a valid reason. These reasons include improper or unethical conduct, conflicts of interest, and malpractice. However, you cannot change lawyers merely to stall for time.

If you are dissatisfied with your lawyer's conduct or the way the matter is progressing, consult another lawyer for an opinion. Do this *before* taking action, because you need a professional opinion to know whether your lawyer acted correctly or improperly. Never fire your lawyer until you have hired a replacement. Otherwise, you may be unrepresented, and your case could accidentally be dismissed. If you fire your lawyer, you may be required to pay for the work rendered. You may also have to go to court to settle the issue of legal fees. However, this should not stop you from taking action if it's warranted.

You have the right to change lawyers at any time if there is a valid reason.

If you have evidence that your lawyer misused your funds for personal gain or committed fraud, immediately file a complaint with the grievance committee of your state or local bar association. All complaints are confidential, and you cannot be sued for filing a complaint if it is later determined that the lawyer did nothing wrong. In some states, clients can be reimbursed up to $100,000 for funds stolen by lawyers.

In New York, for example, the state legislature has enacted a Lawyer's Fund for Client Protection. All practicing lawyers in the state are required to pay an annual registration fee of approximately $100 for use by the fund. When lawyers bilk clients out of money due (e.g., money given by the client to the lawyer for security deposits in real estate transactions, money paid by insurance companies to lawyers on behalf of their clients for personal injury settlements, etc.), administrators of the fund determine who is entitled to receive reimbursement and for how much (up to a $100,000 limit).

Most states have enacted similar plans to protect consumers from disreputable lawyers, since the number and size of client complaints has increased dramatically. In New York, for example, $2.6 million in awards to 104 bilked clients was awarded in the 1991–92 year. Many of the awards were made to clients cheated by one lawyer! However, in most of these states you are *not* entitled to reimbursement for any money misused or lost by your attorney engaged in a business transaction with you as a partner; you are entitled to reimbursement only for money lost as a client.

Another alternative is to commence a malpractice suit against your lawyer. Legal malpractice arises when a lawyer fails to use "such skill or prudence as lawyers of ordinary skill commonly possess and experience in the performance of the tasks they undertake." This doesn't mean that you can sue if your lawyer loses your case. You can sue only if he or she fails to render work or assistance of *minimal competence* and you are damaged as a result. You can also sue for malpractice when there is a breach of ethics (such as the failure to remit funds belonging to a client) in addition to suit for breach of contract and/or civil fraud.

Speak to another lawyer before embarking on any of these courses of action.

The following are examples of lawyer malpractice:

- settling a case without your consent
- procrastinating (e.g., neglecting to prepare a will and the client dies)
- charging improper fees
- failing to file a claim within the requisite time period (the statue of limitations)
- failing to competently and aggressively represent you in a criminal matter
- failing to inform you of a material point to your detriment (e.g., neglecting to advise you or failing to include language in a separation agreement giving the wife a portion of her husband's military pension in a divorce settlement in a community property state)

Should You Appeal a Case?

The vast majority of lawsuits never go to trial; they are discontinued or settled. However, every case that is tried has a loser, and the losing party must decide whether to appeal the decision. Talk to your lawyer immediately if you receive an unfavorable verdict. You have a limited period of time in which you can file a notice that you intend to appeal.

The appeals process works this way: Appeals judges read the transcript of the trial, together with legal documents (called "briefs"), to determine if the trial judge or jury erred in their decision. *This rarely happens.* Less than 20 percent of all criminal cases and 30 percent of all civil cases are reversed on appeal. However, some decisions are reversed. If you have spent several years and thousands of dollars pursuing or defending a valid claim, the additional money spent for an appeal may be worthwhile (particularly if the delay caused by the appeal process works to your advantage).

To evaluate the chances of a successful appeal, carefully reconstruct the reasons why you lost the case. You must also decide whether to hire your present lawyer or one who specializes in appeal matters. Although your lawyer is familiar with your case, there is much to be said for hiring a lawyer who makes his or her living writing briefs and arguing appeals.

Be certain you know how much the appeal will cost, and sign a new agreement that spells out lawyer fees, costs, and disbursements.

DEALING WITH A FINANCIAL ADVISER

Financial planning is a multibillion-dollar industry made up of hundreds of thousands of individual and small partnerships with a few big brokerage firms and insurance companies. Services typically include recommending investment strategies and advising clients on the best financial products (stocks and bonds, mutual funds, insurance policies, and annuities) to buy. Fees are earned for creating long-term investment strategies and take the form of flat fees ($500–$20,000) for setting up and overseeing a plan, an hourly charge ($75–$400) for work performed, commissions (ranging from one-quarter of 1 percent of the investment placed to 100 percent of the first year's premium for a life insurance policy), or a combination.

There is no federal and little state regulation of financial planners. These people are not required to pass exams demonstrating minimum competence such as those required for CPAs and lawyers. Although planners who offer investment advice are required to register with the Securities and Exchange Commission (SEC) and pay a small fee, there is little

Amanda inherited a significant amount of assets from her mother's estate. At the funeral she was introduced to a man whose card identified him as a "financial planner." Eager to invest her inheritance, Amanda did not meet the planner at his office and forgot to discuss and confirm the financial planner's fees in writing. She also did not take the time to investigate the man's credentials.

The man advised Amanda to invest some of the money in a tax shelter that was later disallowed by the IRS, costing her penalties and interest. Eventually, it was discovered that the man failed to provide her with receipts of purchases and had stolen some of the money earmarked for other investments.

protection from disreputable individuals. Follow these strategies before hiring any financial planner.

1. Investigate the planner's credentials, including educational background and affiliation with professional organizations. (For example, does the planner have a master's degree in finance or business?) Many professional associations, including the Institute of Certified Financial Planners, the National Association for Financial Planning, and the International Association of Financial Planning, require extensive skills and qualifications before accepting members. In fact, as a first step, it is a good idea to contact one of the leading associations for a referral of several planners located near you to interview.
2. Ask for the names of satisfied clients as references. Speak to these people in depth to get a better picture of how the planner operates.
3. Get personal recommendations from business associates, friends, and relatives who have successfully used a financial consultant.
4. Understand your needs and select a financial planner accordingly. Do you need a specialist in, say, retirement or estate planning, or do you want a generalist? Choose a planner who understands your financial objectives and investment philosophy.

5. Insist on a written agreement disclosing what services will be rendered and how fees will be earned. Avoid arrangements where the financial planner makes money simply by implementing his or her recommendations; this may show a conflict of interest.

Insist on the following protections before implementing your financial plan:

- You do not give your money directly to the financial planner but to the company, bank, or institution whose assets you are purchasing or acquiring. This prevents the planner from taking your money and failing to turn it over to the appropriate entity.
- You will invest only in deals where the money is insured.
- The financial planner sends regular, accurate statements so you can keep track of your investments.
- The planner cannot make decisions without your approval.
- The planner does not have power of attorney to sign documents on your behalf.

Dealing with a Stockbroker

Most people are more interested in selecting a stockbroker to enhance profits than in knowing and enforcing their rights as an investor. However, there are common industry abuses that all investors should be aware of.

- churning (excessive trading to earn increased commissions)
- mutual fund switching that results in excessive sales loads
- charging unauthorized transactions to an account
- charging excessive commissions and illegal markups
- giving illegal and unenforceable guarantees against losses
- making false sales presentations
- insider trading
- allowing and even encouraging investors to participate in legal but risky stock option trading

One of the first things to consider when hiring a stockbroker is the kind of services you want. Broker-dealers, also known as brokerage firms or securities dealers, typically provide full clerical support and supervision for the individual brokers working for them. There are three types of brokerage firms:

1. The full-service brokerage offers a variety of services, from effectuating stock and bond purchases, options and commodities trades to offering internal financial products such as mutual funds, securities, and syndications. People hiring stockbrokers who work for full-service brokerage firms will usually pay larger commissions. Such brokers typically work on a commission basis and often share their earnings with the house, which is providing the overhead and technical and research support.
2. The discount broker working for a discount brokerage firm usually charges a lower commission or fee for a stock trade because typically the broker is paid a salary rather than commission. All you are paying for is the execution of a buy or sell order. Discount brokerage firms do not engage in financial analysis and research; this is reflected in the lower fees.
3. Specialized brokers offer lower fees for other financial products depending on their specialty. For example, some specialized brokerages sell only mutual funds; thus, if you wanted to purchase a share of a particular mutual fund, you would pay a lower fee than you would to a full-service brokerage firm.

Minimizing Risk

When contemplating investment opportunities, always consider your age, financial goals, current financial situation, ability to take risk, and long-term financial outlook. Never put all of your funds in one investment; diversify to reduce the chance of loss.

Understand the tax consequences of your investment, since taxes can play a large part of the bottom line. In fact, your broker-dealer must report all information to the IRS and send you a 1099 form indicating the exact amount of interest and dividends you earned in a given year.

Smart investors request written materials from the companies they wish to purchase *and* recommendation letters from the broker that spell out the pros and cons of the investment recommendations. Remember, most brokers are salespeople who earn bonuses based on volume of sales.

Experts suggest that by demanding written information and a written analysis of a proposed transaction, you will present yourself as a serious and careful investor and reduce the chance your broker will take advantage of you. If your broker refuses to give you a written recommendation because he has no time or the request is unusual, consider working with someone else.

Ask the stockbroker you are considering for references. Meet with the individual at his or her office. Ask questions about his or her title and the professional associations he or she belongs to. Has the broker passed the series of examinations required by the National Association of Securities Dealers (NASD)? How much experience and training does the person have? Check the broker's disciplinary record. The NASD maintains a file on serious disciplinary violations committed by stockbrokers. You can receive an information request form and obtain this information by calling 301-590-6500.

Most important, learn the broker's standard operating procedure. Does he or she understand your investment philosophy? Who will handle your account when he or she is on vacation or sick? You should also inquire how quickly you will receive your money after a trade has been consummated. Speak to and meet the broker's manager and ask about the firm's procedures for handling customer complaints.

To avoid exploitation, be sure to get a written agreement spelling out proposed fees and conduct. Never allow a broker to make unauthorized trades on your account. Keep meticulous written records documenting dates, times, and the substance of conversations with your broker and the actual deals authorized. In addition, review and save all documents you sign when opening a brokerage account. For example, a new-account form lists essential information about you and your investment objectives and should detail fair and appropriate trading. The new-account form is typically signed by the brokerage firm's representative (the person with whom you deal) and by the registered representative's branch manager. This and other forms may help you later in the case of churning, excessively risky trading, or lack of supervision.

When you hire a stockbroker, send a letter confirming the investment strategy chosen and describing what you have and have not authorized the broker to do on your behalf.

Finally, be aware that some brokers try to sell stocks over the telephone to people who are not their regular customers. Never purchase stocks in this manner. Always deal with your own, established stockbroker after you have personally visited with the broker several times and feel comfortable with his or her philosophy. Never make stock decisions from offering literature sent to you by a broker you don't know personally.

> *Jack forwarded $100,000 to his stockbroker with instructions to invest the money in prudent, safe stocks. Jack was called out of the country on business for three months and failed to call his broker during that time. When he returned, he learned that his stockbroker had made 21 transactions on his behalf, netting a loss of $42,000. Jack commenced an arbitration against the broker and his firm, alleging churning (excessive trading) among other causes of action. At the trial he proved that (1) the trading done in his account was excessive in light of his investment objectives; (2) the broker exercised unauthorized control over the trading of the account; and (3) the broker acted with intent to defraud or with willful and reckless disregard for the interests of his client. The arbitrators ruled that the number of speculative trades was prompted by selfish concerns to earn the broker excessive commissions.*

Resolving Problems with Your Broker

Investors have legal rights upon opening an account with a broker-dealer. These include the right to be kept informed regarding all trades that are made and to receive copies of all executed trades with complete documentation confirming these transactions. Investors have the right not to be given fraudulent information and not to be misrepresented. You also have the right not to be sold more than you can afford or encouraged to speculate in risky ventures. The broker is obligated to follow your instructions exactly and completely. Finally, the broker-dealer owes investors the highest degree of loyalty and good faith.

If a financial professional commits a fraudulent act that results in monetary damage, you should consider taking the following steps:

- complain directly to the broker
- complain to the manager of the brokerage house
- complain to the New York Stock Exchange (NYSE), the American Stock Exchange, or the NASD
- complain to the SEC

The first way to resolve a dispute with your broker is by telephone. Discuss the matter in detail and send a letter by certified mail, return receipt requested, documenting your complaint. Also send a copy of this letter by certified mail, return receipt requested, to the manager of the brokerage firm. If the matter is not resolved to your immediate satisfaction by the broker or the manager, send a final demand letter by certified mail, return receipt requested, that states that stronger action will be taken immediately. If you haven't lost money but you want to lodge a complaint against the broker or the firm, you can register your complaint with the District Business Conduct Committee of the NASD. The committee can bring an enforcement proceeding and impose sanctions if the broker-dealer is guilty of misconduct.

At any stage of the complaint you may decide to hire an attorney to protect or enforce your rights. This should always be considered, particularly if the amount in dispute or your losses exceed $10,000. However, you may be able to obtain recompense without the expense of hiring an attorney by filing a claim with the enforcement sections of the SEC, NYSE, or NASD. Small-claims arbitration (for disputes involving less than $10,000) is available through the NASD. Information regarding many of the options available can be obtained by calling the NASD at 202-728-8000 or 212-858-4000, and the NYSE at 212-656-3000.

It is often a good idea to speak to a knowledgeable securities lawyer—that is, a lawyer who specializes in securities law—to consider all your options. He or she can tell you how to prove a case of broker fraud, what damages you may be entitled to receive, which forum is the best area to resolve your matter via legal recourse, and whether you are bound to litigate your matter through arbitration. Most forms and agreements that broker-dealers require their customers to sign contain a clause binding investors to arbitration. A knowledgeable securities attorney can advise if this applies to you.

AVOIDING PROBLEMS WITH HOMEOWNER'S AND PROPERTY INSURANCE

The average consumer spends 12 cents out of every income dollar on insurance. Often, however, people do not understand the coverage they are receiving, fail to interpret onerous clauses in their insurance contracts, and have trouble collecting insurance proceeds from their carrier.

When purchasing insurance, one of the best ways to compare policies in price and coverage is simply to call various insurance agents and ask about a particular policy. Speak to friends, relatives, and business associates to find out what they are receiving and how much they are paying. You can also contact your local state department of insurance office for information on a company's fees and any complaints filed against them.

> *To obtain reports and rating guides containing financial and other important information on all insurance companies doing business in the United States, contact A.M. Best Company, Oldwick, N.J. 08858; (201) 439-2200.*

Buying a Homeowner's Policy

- Read the insurance application and proposed policy carefully. Be aware of exclusions clauses, which limit the insurance company's responsibility to pay. These are typically written in bold print but are often confusing. It is essential to know what coverage you will *not* receive before you buy an insurance policy. For example, does your homeowner's policy provide adequate coverage in the event of a natural disaster, like a hurricane or tornado? What about damage caused from floods, fire, rain, or lightning?
- Complete the application truthfully. Companies regularly deny coverage for insurance on the basis that prior conditions or

problems existed but were not revealed. This is called "material misrepresentation" or "omission."

- Pay premiums on time. Late payments may give the insurance company the opportunity to deny a claim or cancel your policy. If the premiums are too expensive, consider obtaining a policy with a higher deductible rather than buy less insurance.
- Maintain a complete inventory of all belongings insured for homeowner's and property insurance policies, and keep a separate copy outside of your home. In fact, experts suggest that it is a good idea to have a video or pictures taken of all possessions you wish to be covered. Better still, draw a floor plan of each room of your house and include in the plan the contents of each room.
- Save your sales receipts to prove the value of covered property.
- Review your insurance policy regularly to determine if gaps exist because of changed circumstances. For example, should you buy replacement-cost coverage, which pays to replace the home without regard to its age or condition, or the standard actual cash-value coverage, which is cheaper but pays just the replacement cost minus depreciation? The most expensive policy to obtain is guaranteed-replacement cost coverage, which will compensate you to rebuild your home even when the new cost exceeds the value of the policy.
- And unless you purchased a rider to the policy (sometimes called a floater) for personal possessions and valuables—including expensive jewelry, furs, and paintings—you may not receive anything near the value of these items from the policy upon their loss.

Filing a Claim

- Never file false claims or exaggerate your loss.
- Contact your adjuster before filing a claim to determine what you are entitled to under the policy and the best way to prove the extent of your losses.
- File a claim immediately.
- File a police report immediately in the event of an accident, theft, or break-in—the report will be evidence and proof of your loss when filing an insurance claim.

- Take photographs of damaged property before and after it is repaired. It is also a good idea to take color photographs of recent injuries when filing accident claims and disability claims.
- Maintain complete records of repair and replacement costs, medical bills, and so forth. Pay by check; the canceled check will serve as proof of payment.
- Save all repair estimates, bills, receipts, proof of payment, and pertinent documents.

How to Collect on Your Claim

- Contact your insurance company immediately in writing if you have difficulty collecting on your policy. Draft the letter carefully since it may be used as evidence of the insurance company's lack of diligence in handling your claim. In fact, it may be wise to have an attorney analyze your case and write the letter if a large amount of money is claimed.
- Seek legal and other professional advice if your insurance company refuses to pay for your loss. Insurance companies frequently err in their analysis of written policies and their duty to pay the customer for a loss covered under a policy, including payment for repairs made to avoid further damage or for reasonable living expenses if the property is unlivable due to the damage caused by a storm or natural disaster. As a last resort, you might consider filing a lawsuit based on breach of contract or negligence.
- File a grievance with your state's insurance department. Most state insurance departments investigate complaints against insurance companies, brokers, agents, and adjusters, and many attempt to mediate disputes regarding premiums, coverage, and renewals. When amicable attempts to resolve matters fail, these agencies can commence formal investigations and hearings on a consumer's behalf, particularly when a certain aspect of an insurance company's conduct has affected many consumers (a class action).
- Hire a public adjuster to help you prepare your property damage claim. For a fee (up to one-third of the additional money recovered through their efforts but usually up to 10 percent of the amount received), public adjusters often interpret your policy, secure estimates, and take inventory of your losses. They may be worth

the money in difficult situations where a substantial sum is involved. Since fees vary, negotiate the fee to be paid; some adjusters may even accept an hourly rate. The best public adjusters typically belong to reputable associations such as the National Association of Public Insurance Adjusters. Obtain references, detailed work experience, and professional affiliations before hiring the adjuster, and demand a written agreement that states fees to be charged and services to be performed.

Never automatically accept an unfavorable insurance company decision if you believe the denial of your claim was unfair.

- Never automatically accept an unfavorable insurance company decision if you believe the denial of your claim was unfair. Acceptance may constitute settlement of the claim in full.

Locating an Insurance Company That Has Gone Out of Business

Visit the company's previous location to see if there is a sign for a new address. Check with nearby firms and the building landlord to see if they know of the company's whereabouts.

Send a certified letter, return receipt requested, to the firm at its last-known address. The return receipt will show if the letter was forwarded and to whom it was delivered.

Call the post office and telephone company for any forwarding instructions.

Contact the federal bankruptcy court in the county where the main office of the company was located to learn if the company filed for bankruptcy.

AVOIDING UNNECESSARY FUNERAL COSTS AND RIP-OFFS

The cost of an average funeral can easily exceed $4,000. To find out where you can obtain a low-cost funeral in your community, call a memorial society. Most societies provide nonmembers with information about the types of services available and comparative costs. Look under "Memorial Society" or "Funeral Society" in the Yellow Pages. If there is no such society in your community, one in a nearby city may know of undertakers in your area who provide low- or reasonable-cost funerals. You can also speak to clergy at a church or synagogue for recommendations. Finally, some labor union committees, consumer groups, civic organizations, and fraternal societies can be helpful. It is best to make as many arrangements as possible before the need arises.

Recognize the low-cost alternatives to a conventional funeral. Substantial costs can be saved through cremation, direct burial, and organ donation. Many crematories charge only several hundred dollars to cremate a body. Direct burial through commercial businesses can also offer substantial savings. Some alternatives to conventional funerals may even be covered by the social security death benefit available to most Americans.

The Law

Until recently, few federal and state laws existed to protect consumers from being victimized by unscrupulous operators. Most funeral establishments had no set methods of pricing, and many consumers emotionally unprepared for the death of a loved one could not protect themselves as well as an educated consumer in this area. A host of abuses resulted, especially when funeral establishments regularly lumped all services into one price and consumers paid for unnecessary or unwarranted items.

To combat many abuses in the industry, the Federal Trade Commission enacted legislation to protect consumers from unfair and deceptive practices. Generally, the FTC's Funeral Rule 16 CFR 453 requires that funeral providers nationwide give consumers a written, itemized list that contains the prices of funeral goods and services. This list must be offered at the beginning of any discussion of funeral arrangements in person and even over the telephone to those consumers who request information about the terms, conditions, and prices at which funeral goods and services are offered by that funeral home.

The following are some of the services for which you should request itemization:

- professional staff services
- embalming
- cosmetology
- general use of facilities
- use of facilities for funeral services
- initial transfer of deceased to funeral home
- hearse
- acknowledgment cards
- visitor register
- coffin
- cemetery plot

The rule also requires that funeral providers

1. obtain express permission from a family member or representative before charging a fee for embalming, except under special circumstances
2. not require consumers to purchase a casket for use in a direct cremation service
3. offer an alternative to a traditional casket
4. not misrepresent legal requirements for burial or cremation (such as erroneous but expensive and unnecessary state and local laws about embalming, caskets for cremation, cemetery, and other regulations)
5. not misrepresent the existence of markups on cash advance items (i.e., that items such as flowers are sold to customers at cost when this is not true)

Certain unfair practices are also prohibited, such as conditioning the purchase of any funeral good or service on the purchase of any other funeral good or service.

Since a few states have enacted laws even tougher than the FTC funeral rule, a funeral provider in your state is required to honor either your state's law or the FTC funeral rule, whichever law is stronger. Be aware that funeral providers are defined as any person, partnership, or corporation that sells or offers to sell funeral goods (e.g., all products sold to the public for use in connection with funeral services) and funeral services (e.g., those services used to care for and prepare human bodies for burial or other disposition and those services used to arrange, supervise, or conduct the funeral or disposition, such as a cemetery that also operates a funeral home). The rule's coverage extends to funeral providers who sell pre-need contracts for goods and services.

Other areas of protection require that a funeral provider not tell a consumer that embalming is required when the consumer wishes immediate burial, when the remains are placed in a sealed casket, or when refrigeration is available. A general price list for all storage containers must be provided. Additionally, the family should be told that certain price items apply for direct cremations but that other fees are required for cremations that occur after a viewing.

To avoid problems, never agree on a service when the price for that item appears high. Never pay for extra goods or services (such as burial clothing, flowers, etc.) that were not discussed with you and that you did not agree to pay for before the funeral.

Resolving a Dispute

In many states, funeral homes are licensed by the health department. In other states, the department of consumer affairs is responsible for investigating matters under dispute and conducting formal hearings. Both agencies often attempt to resolve complaints informally. However, if attempts at settling your complaint are unsuccessful, fines can be imposed and licenses suspended or revoked for blatant violations.

Given the broad powers of the Federal Trade Commission, *always* advise the funeral provider in a registered letter that you will be contacting the regional office of the Federal Trade Commission's Investigation Division by filing a complaint and requesting an investigation in the event the matter is not immediately resolved to your satisfaction. Most funeral providers are reluctant to tangle with the FTC and "open their books" during an investigation, so your problem may be amicably resolved.

If you do not receive immediate satisfaction, contact the nearest FTC regional office by telephone and speak to an investigator. Follow this up by sending a letter of protest (certified mail, return receipt requested) to document your problem and seek redress.

If you are the victim of misrepresentation or other fraud, you can also sue the funeral director and establishment in small claims court when the amount in dispute is less than $2,500. Of course, you should consider hiring a lawyer to pursue your rights if the amount is larger.

Survivors' Benefits

The following are some of the benefits that may be available to survivors upon application:

- employment benefits—severance pay, accrued vacation, golden parachute and golden coffin benefits, stock options and appreciation rights, insurance death benefits, pension and profit-sharing distributions
- social security and Veterans Administration benefits
- worker's compensation insurance benefits
- credit union, trade union, and fraternal organization benefits
- federal, state, and local government survivors' benefits
- no-fault automobile insurance benefits to cover funeral and burial expenses for someone killed in an auto accident
- Federal Railroad Retirement Board benefits for railroad employees

FIGURE 6.1 Sample Living Will/Health Proxy

I, (name of individual), currently residing at (address), being of sound mind and health, hereby make known my directions to my family, friends, all physicians, hospitals and other health-care providers and any Court or Judge:

After thoughtful consideration, I have decided to forgo all life-sustaining treatment if I shall sustain substantial and irreversible loss of mental capacity and my attending physician is of the opinion that I am unable to eat and drink without medical assistance and it is highly unlikely that I will regain the ability to eat and drink without medical assistance; or my attending physician is of the opinion that I have an incurable or irreversible condition that is likely to cause my death within a relatively short time.

I shall be conclusively presumed to have sustained an irreversible loss of mental capacity upon a determination to such effect by my attending physician or when a Court determines that I have sustained such loss, whichever shall first occur.

As used herein, the term "an incurable or irreversible condition which is likely to cause my death within a relatively short time" is a condition which, without the administration of medical procedures, would serve only to prolong the process of dying and will, in my attending physician's opinion, result in my death within a relatively short period of time. The determination as to whether my death would occur in a relatively short period of time is to be made by my attending physician without considering the possibilities of extending my life with life-sustaining treatment.

I direct that this decision shall be carried into effect even if I am unable to personally reconfirm or communicate it, without seeking judicial approval or authority. Accordingly, if and when it is so determined that (1) I have sustained substantial and irreversible loss of mental capacity and (2) I am unable to eat and drink without medical assistance and it is highly unlikely that I will regain the capacity to eat and drink without medical assistance or I have an incurable or irreversible condition which is likely to cause my death within a relatively short time, all life-sustaining treatment (including without limitation, administration of nourishment and liquids intravenously or by tubes connected to my digestive tract) shall thereupon be withheld or withdrawn forthwith, whether or not I am conscious, alert, or free from pain, and no cardiopulmonary resuscitation shall thereafter be administered to me if I sustain cardiac or pulmonary arrest. In such circumstances I consent to an order not to resuscitate, as that term is defined in New York Public Health Law Section 2961, and direct that such an order thereupon be placed in my medical record. I recognize that when life-sustaining treatment is withheld or withdrawn from me, I will surely die of dehydration and malnutrition within days or weeks. All available medication for the relief of pain and for my comfort shall be administered to me after life-sustaining treatment is withheld or withdrawn, even if I am rendered unconscious and my life is shortened thereby.

I wish to die at home and not in a hospital, and I do not want to be transferred to a hospital unless my condition makes it impractical for me to be treated at home, as may be the case during severe hemorrhage, or extreme restlessness, convulsions, or unmanageable pain; in which case, then as soon as possible, I want to be sent back home.

I recognize that there may be many instances besides those described above in which the compassionate practice of good medicine dictates that life-sustaining treatment be withheld or withdrawn, and I do not intend that this instrument be construed as an exclusive enumeration of the circumstances in which I have decided to forgo life-sustaining treatment. To the contrary, it is my express direction that whenever the compassionate practice of good medicine dictates that life-sustaining treatment should not be administered, such treatment shall be withheld or withdrawn from me. I similarly direct that in the event I am able to personally communicate a decision to forgo life-sustaining treatment in other circumstances than those described herein, such instructions shall be followed to the same extent as if originally included in this declaration.

This instrument and the instructions herein contained may be revoked by me at any time and in any manner. However, no physician, hospital, or other health-care provider who withholds or withdraws life-sustaining treatment in reliance upon this Living Will or upon my personally communicated instructions without actual knowledge that I have countermanded these instructions shall have any liability or responsibility to me, my estate, or any other person for having withheld such treatment.

I am in full command of my faculties. I make this Living Will declaration in order to furnish clear and convincing proof of the strength and durability of my determination to forgo life-sustaining treatment in the circumstances described above. I emphasize my firm and settled conviction that I am entitled to forgo such treatment in the exercise of my right to determine the course of my medical treatment. My right to forgo such treatment is paramount to any responsibility of any health-care provider or the authority of any Court or Judge to attempt to force unwanted medical care upon me.

I direct that my family, friends, all physicians, hospitals and other health-care providers and any Court or Judge honor my decision that my life not be artificially extended by mechanical means and that if there is any doubt as to whether or not life-sustaining treatment is to be administered to me after I have sustained substantial and irreversible loss of mental capacity, such doubt is to be resolved in favor of withholding or withdrawing such treatment.

I have discussed this document with (names of witnesses), and I appoint said (name of individual) as my Surrogate and Health Proxy to act for me in any and all of the within premises, and if any interpretation of this document is ever necessary, my said Surrogate and Health Proxy is authorized to interpret it.

_____
(Name)

Dated: (Place of execution), February   , 199 .

WITNESS:_____
ADDRESS:_____

WITNESS:_____
ADDRESS:_____

WITNESS:_____
ADDRESS:_____

STATE OF NEW YORK   )
) SS.:
COUNTY OF NEW YORK)

On this (date), before me personally appeared (person's name), to me known to me to be the individual described in and who executed the foregoing instrument, and she acknowledged to me that she executed the same.

_____

Notary Public

FIGURE 6.2 **Sample Retainer Agreement**

Date

Jane Doe (Client)
Anyplace, U.S.A.

Re: Retainer Agreement Regarding Doe vs. Doe

Dear Jane Doe:

This letter confirms that you have retained me as your attorney to negotiate a settlement agreement with your husband, if that is reasonably possible; or, if not, to represent you in a divorce action. You agree to pay to me
promptly an initial retainer of $1,500, which is my minimum fee in this mat-
ter. If I devote more than 10 hours to this case based upon my time records
commencing from the initial conference, you shall pay an additional fee
counted at the rate of $150/hour.

If you should decide to discontinue my services in this matter at any time,
you shall be liable for my time computed at the rate of $150/hour.

These fees do not include any work in appellate courts, any other actions
or proceedings, or out-of-pocket disbursements. Out-of-pocket disbursements include but are not limited to costs of filing papers, court fees, process
servers, witness fees, court reporters, long-distance telephone calls, travel,
parking, and photocopies normally made by me or requested by you, which
disbursements shall be paid for or reimbursed to me upon my request.

You are aware of the hazards of litigation and that, despite my efforts on
your behalf, there is no assurance or guarantee of the outcome of this
matter.

Kindly indicate your understanding and acceptance of the above by signing this letter below where indicated. I look forward to serving you.

Sincerely yours,
(Signature)

I have read and understand the above letter, have received a copy, and
accept all of its terms:

_____

Jane Doe

FIGURE 6.3 **Sample Contingency Fee Arrangement**

Date

John Doe (Client)
Anyplace, U.S.A.

Re: Retainer Agreement
      Regarding Doe vs. Smith

Dear John Doe:

This letter confirms that we will represent you in the prosecution of your claim for personal injuries sustained by you on February 16, 1993, as a result of an auto accident with Mr. Smith in Cleveland, Ohio.

We will devote our efforts to this matter for a fee, the amount of which will depend upon the outcome of your claim:

1. If nothing is recovered, you will not be indebted to us for our services.

2. If we are successful, we will receive 25 percent of the amount obtained for you if no suit is filed, and 33⅓ percent of any amount recovered after suit is filed.

3. Actual costs expended in reaching a settlement, if any, are to be paid by you.

4. Proceeds, if any, recovered by way of settlement judgment, or otherwise shall be disbursed as follows: All our costs which have not been reimbursed by you will be deducted; our fees, as set out in the percentage above, will be deducted and the balance will be paid to you.

5. Should you decide to discharge us and retain another law firm, we shall receive a reasonable percentage of the proceeds recovered by said firm as fees for our services.

If this letter correctly states our understanding, will you please so indicate by signing this agreement in the space provided below and returning it to us.

Sincerely yours,

_____

John Doe

FIGURE 6.4 Sample Monthly Billing Statement

Date

Name of Client
Company
Address

Current statement for all services rendered in the matter of the contract negotiation between (name of client) and (name of employer) at the rate of $200 per hour per agreement:

1.	1/05/94	Tel. conv. with Employer's Attorney 9:40–9:45 a.m.	5 min.
		Tel. conv. with Client 9:15–9:20 a.m.	5 min.
		Tel. conv. with Client 12:10–12:15 p.m.	5 min.
2.	1/04/94	Draft of Revised Agreement including tel. conv. with Client 6:50–8:05 a.m.	75 min.
3.	1/03/94	Meeting with Client 1:40–2:50 p.m.	70 min.
4.	12/19/93	Review of initial proposed Agreement 7:30–7:55 a.m.	25 min.
		Tel. conv. with Client 9:35–9:40 a.m.; 3:40–3:45 p.m.	10 min.

Total time spent on Matter from December 19, 1993 through January 5, 1994 at standard rate of $200 per hour:

195 min. or 3.25 hours

Amount earned: $650.00

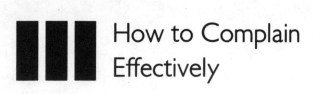

How to Complain Effectively

7 Obtaining Satisfaction and Recompense

The most effective way to complain is in a reasonable and friendly fashion: Don't initially make demands. Presenting your complaint in person is often more successful than complaining over the telephone. In either case, always record the person's full name and title and the date and time of the conversation. Then write a letter to that person, thanking him or her and confirming when and how the matter is to be resolved.

Savvy consumers always first attempt to negotiate solutions to their problems. They also have figured out their next step. If you are having trouble getting through to an employee, speak to his or her boss. Go directly to the owner or president of an establishment if you are being ignored or encountering unnecessary delays. Be persistent when dealing with large companies or bureaucracies and get the names of everyone you deal with. Finally, know the law and which agency is authorized to protect your rights if your problem is still unresolved.

> **Savvy consumers always first attempt to negotiate solutions to their problems.**

Whenever you have a consumer problem, write a demand letter and send it certified mail, return receipt requested. The importance of sending such a letter cannot be overemphasized. In addition to documenting your claim, the letter will advise your adversary that the matter must be corrected to your immediate satisfaction or you will take additional action. If there is no response to your letter, send a follow-up letter reporting that your initial letter has not been answered. The letter should also state what your next step will be if this letter is ignored.

STRATEGIES TO WIN YOUR CASE IN SMALL CLAIMS COURT

If you cannot get satisfaction by personal negotiation, you might consider suing in small claims court.

Small claims courts, which help you collect money in an informal and inexpensive manner *without* hiring a lawyer, hear over a million cases a year. They can be used in many situations. For example, you may wish to sue for money damages when:

- your employer fails to pay you
- someone damages your property and refuses to pay for repairs
- a car dealer refuses to return a refundable deposit when you cancel the deal
- you purchase merchandise that is damaged during delivery and the store refuses to replace it or refund your money
- you want to recover money you paid to a mechanic who does shoddy work or gives poor service
- you are a victim of misleading advertising
- a dry cleaning establishment ruins your clothing

Small claims court works. Many have night sessions and matters are resolved quickly, sometimes within a month from the time an action is filed. The maximum amount of money you can recover varies from state to state. It is usually up to $2,500.

The following guidelines describe the procedures of a typical small claims court. However, the rules vary in each city and state. Before you contemplate starting a lawsuit, call the clerk of that court and ask for a written explanation of the specific procedural rules to be followed.

Who Can Be Sued?

Small claims court can be used to sue any person, business, partnership, corporation, or government body owing you money. If you sue in small claims court and recover a judgment, you are precluded from suing again to recover any additional money owed to you. Thus, if your claim greatly exceeds the maximum amount of money that might be awarded in small claims court, consider hiring a lawyer and instituting suit in a higher court.

Small claims court can be used to sue any person, business, partnership, corporation, or government body owing you money.

Do You Have a Valid Claim?

In order to be successful, you must have a valid claim. This means that you must:

1. identify the person or business that damaged or caused you harm
2. calculate the amount of damages you suffered
3. show that there is some basis in law to have a court award you damages
4. be sure that you were not the main cause of your own harm, that you haven't waited too long to start the action (statute of limitations), and that you did not sign a written release

The fact that you have been damaged physically or monetarily does not mean that you will automatically recover money damages in small claims court. For example, suppose you are assaulted after striking someone, are involved in an automobile accident that you could have avoided, or receive a check that bounces after you fail to deliver goods as promised. Chances are you cannot recover money for your loss.

Where to Sue

Call your local bar association, city hall, or the county courthouse to discover where the nearest small claims court is located. (In some states, small claims court is called justice court, district court, municipal court, or justice of the peace court.) You cannot start the action just anyplace. In most states, suit must be brought in the county in which the person or business you are suing lives or does business.

Confirm this with the small claims court clerk and ask what days and hours the court is in session. Also find out the maximum amount of money you can sue for, what documents are needed to file a complaint, the filing fee, and whether this can be paid by cash, check, or money order.

What Can You Sue For?

You can sue only to collect *money*. If you purchased a defective dishwasher and seek replacement, the court does not have the power to order the store to give you another dishwasher. But if you win your case, you will be awarded money to buy another one. Thus, before you begin to sue in small claims court, estimate the loss in money you wish to collect.

Sometimes you need not have spent money before starting an action. For example, you can sue in small claims court when a car dealer refuses to honor a warranty, which will force you to spend money to have your car repaired. (Obtain written estimates from local merchants to *prove* your *claim*.) Or, you may have been promised that a new stereo system would be delivered to your house the day before a party and the unit never arrived. (Calculate a monetary figure for the damage you sustained as a result of the nondelivery.)

When calculating the amount of your claim, include all incurred expenses, including gasoline bills, tolls, telephone costs, losses due to time missed from work, sales tax, and interest, if applicable. Save all your receipts for this purpose.

Starting the Lawsuit

You begin the lawsuit by paying a small fee (about $4) and either going to the court in person or mailing in a complaint that states the following information:

- your name and address
- the complete name and address of the person, business, or company you are suing (the defendant)

- the amount of money you believe you are owed
- the facts
- the reasons you (the plaintiff) are seeking redress

If you are filing a claim on behalf of an individually owned business, you must list the name of the owner in addition to the name of the business. If you are filing a claim on behalf of a partnership, you must list the name of the partnership as the plaintiff. (Some states do not allow a corporation to sue someone in small claims court.)

Be sure to write the accurate and complete name and address of the defendant on the complaint. Write the corporation's formal name rather than its "doing business" (d b/a) name. Thus, if you are suing a corporation, contact the county clerk's office in the county where the corporation does business to obtain its proper name and address. Better still, call the department of corporations in your state to obtain such information.

When you are suing more than one person—for example, a husband and wife—sue each one separately in the complaint. Sue a woman in her legal name rather than her married name (Mary Kane, not Mrs. Mark Kane). If your problem is consumer-oriented, state how you were mistreated. For example, if you demanded satisfaction, or sent a certified letter, specify when and whom you contacted. You might also write, if applicable, that the defendant failed to make you a reasonable offer of settlement after becoming aware of your problem. Some states require you to send a demand letter before suing in small claims court. Investigate this with the clerk (see Figure 7.1).

At this time, you may also be required to prepare another form called a "summons," which notifies your opponent that you are suing him or her. Sometimes the clerk will do this. Ask the clerk whether the court will mail the summons by registered or first-class mail, personally serve the defendant on your behalf, or whether you must hire a professional process server.

If a professional process server is required, ask what is necessary to prove that service was accomplished. You may have to pay the process server an additional fee (between $10 and $30). However, if you win your case, you can ask the judge to include the process server's fee in the award.

When the clerk gives you a hearing date, be sure that it is convenient and you have no other commitments.

The Defendant's Response

When the person or company you are suing receives the summons, the defendant or his or her attorney can:

- deny your claim by mailing a written denial to the court
- deny your claim by personally appearing in court on the day of the hearing
- sue you for money you supposedly owe (this is called a "counterclaim")
- contact you to settle the matter out of court

If an offer of payment is made, ask to be reimbursed for all filing and service costs. Notify the court that you are dismissing the action only *after* you receive payment. (If you are paid by check, wait until it clears.) Do not postpone the case. Tell your opponent that unless you are paid before the day of the trial, you are prepared to go to court and either commence with the trial or stipulate the offer of settlement to the judge.

If a written denial is mailed to the court, ask the clerk to read it to you over the phone or go to the court and read it yourself. This is your right and it may help you prepare for your opponent's defense. The following is an example of a simple denial in an answer:

I deny each and every allegation in the face of the complaint.

Now you must prove your allegations in court to recover your claim.

Your Duties as the Moving Party

It is up to you to follow the progress of your case. Call the clerk and refer to the docket number to discover whether the defendant received the complaint and whether it was answered. If you discover that the defendant did not receive the complaint by the day of the trial, request the clerk to issue a new complaint to be served by a sheriff or process server. Go to court that day anyway, to be sure that the case is not dismissed because of your failure to appear.

If the complaint is personally served and your opponent does not appear at the trial, he or she will be in default and you may be awarded a judgment automatically. In some states, you still have to prove your case in order to be successful. Also, defendants sometimes file motions (legal affidavits) requesting the court to remove the default judgment on the grounds that there was a valid reason for not attending the hearing. If this motion is granted, your trial will be rescheduled.

If you are unable to come to court on the day of the trial, send a certified letter to the clerk, asking for a continuance. The letter should specify the reasons you will be unable to appear and include future dates when you will be able to come to court. *Send a copy of this letter to your opponent.* When you receive a new date, send your opponent a certified letter informing him or her of the revised date.

Requests for continuances are sometimes *not* honored. Call the clerk on the day of the old trial date to be sure that your request has been granted. Be prepared to send a friend or relative to court to ask for a continuance on your behalf if a continuance has not been obtained by the day of the trial.

Preparing for Trial

Subpoenas. You have several weeks to prepare for trial. Use the time wisely. First, be sure that your friendly witnesses, if any, will attend the trial and testify on your behalf. Select witnesses who are believable and who will not say things that will surprise you. In some states, you can present the judge with signed affidavits or statements of witnesses who are unable to appear at the trial. A few states also permit judges to hear testimony via conference telephones.

If necessary, the clerk can issue a subpoena to compel the attendance of important witnesses who you believe may refuse to attend and testify. A subpoena is a document that orders a person to testify or produce books, papers, and other physical objects on a specified date. If the subpoena is issued and the person refuses to appear, a judge can direct a sheriff to bring the witness into court, or even impose a jail sentence for a willful violation of the order.

When you come to court for the trial, check to see if the clerk received any subpoenaed documents. If such records are crucial to your case and have not been received, you can ask for an adjournment. If you have subpoenaed an individual and do not know what he or she looks like, ask the clerk to call out the name to determine if he or she is present so you can proceed with the trial.

Organizing the facts. To maximize your chances of success, organize your case before the day of the trial. Gather and label all of your evidence so that you can produce the documents easily. You may also wish to speak with a lawyer or call a lawyer's referral service for legal advice. Many communities have such advisory organizations, and they are willing to inform you, without charge, about relevant cases and statutes. This may help you know what damages you are legally entitled to. You may cite these laws, if applicable, at the hearing.

Practice what you will say to the judge. This will put you at ease and help you organize the important facts. Make a brief outline and refer to it while speaking. Prepare a list of questions that you would like to ask each witness and your opponent. You are allowed to refer to the list at the hearing.

The Trial

Arrive early, locate the correct courtroom, find the name of your case on the court calendar, and check in with the clerk. You should be properly attired, preferably in business clothes.

Come prepared with all relevant documents. These include:

- receipts and canceled checks
- correspondence
- contracts, leases, and bills of sale
- warranties, advertisements, written promises, and statements made to you
- estimates
- signed affidavits or statements from friends and witnesses unable to appear at the hearing
- clear photographs and other evidence to prove your case
- an employer's statement of lost wages; a doctor's letter reflecting lost time from work
- medical bills and reports

- police and accident reports
- diagrams or charts
- copies of applicable statutes, cases, and regulations
- actual exhibits or products, if possible (For example, if you paid for a new part but a used part was installed in your car, you may wish to bring the used part into court if it can be easily removed and carried.)

When your case is called, you and your opponent will be sworn in. The judge or a court-appointed arbitrator will conduct the hearing and ask you questions. Be relaxed. Keep your presentation brief and to the point. Tell why you are suing the defendant and what you are seeking in money damages. Show your evidence. Bring along a short written summary of the case. You can refer to it during the trial, and if the judge does not come to an immediate decision, he or she can use your outline for reference. Talk directly to the judge and respond to his or her questions. Show respect. Always refer to him or her as "Your Honor" or "Judge." Listen to the judge's instructions and never argue. If the judge asks you a question while you are speaking, stop immediately. Then answer the question honestly and to the point.

Be diplomatic rather than emotional. Also, avoid arguing with your opponent in court and *never* interrupt his or her presentation.

After both sides have finished speaking, you have the opportunity to refute what your opponent told the judge. Do not be intimidated if he or she is accompanied by a lawyer. Simply inform the judge that you are not represented by counsel and are not familiar with small claims court procedures. Ask the judge to intercede on your behalf if you feel that your opponent's attorney is treating you unfairly. Most judges will be sympathetic, since small claims courts are specifically designed for you to present your case without an attorney.

If You Are a Defendant

Follow the same procedures as the plaintiff: prepare your testimony; contact your witnesses to be sure that they will appear at the trial and testify on your behalf; collect your exhibits and documents; arrive early on the day of the trial and check in with the clerk. If you have any doubts about your case, try to settle with the plaintiff before the judge hears the case.

Request that the case be dismissed if your opponent fails to appear. Your adversary will speak first if he or she appears. Wait until he or she is finished speaking before telling your side of the story. Point out any inconsistencies or flaws in your opponent's story. Conclude your remarks by highlighting the important aspects of your case.

Strategies to Help You Win Your Case

Demand letter. Some states require that you send a "30-day demand letter" before filing an action against a retail store or business.

The letter should briefly describe what happened, your money and/or property loss, and what you want the seller or business to do to remedy the situation. Add that you are giving the business 30 days to make a good-faith response. Otherwise, you will begin legal action.

Send the letter certified, return receipt requested, and consider sending copies to your state's attorney general's office, your local consumer protection agency, and the BBB.

If the letter is answered and the business refuses to pay, you may learn what position they intend to take at the trial. If your letter is ignored, that is evidence in court.

Common complaints. The following examples of common complaints illustrate the elements you must prove in court.

Automobile Accident

Example: You are involved in an automobile accident that was not your fault.

What You Must Prove	How to Prove It
1. Time, place, and date of accident	1. Police report, accident report, your testimony, witnesses
2. Facts describing your conduct	2. Your testimony, other witnesses, diagrams, photographs of scene, sketches of street, etc.
3. Facts describing the negligent conduct of your opponent	3. Your testimony, other witnesses, diagrams, sketches of street, etc.

What You Must Prove	*How to Prove It*
4. Damages suffered (a) To automobile	(a) Title or registration, photographs, mechanics' estimates, your testimony, witnesses, itemized repair bills, testimony of mechanic
(b) To you or passengers	(b) Medical bills, employer report showing lost wages, time from work, doctor's report, accident report, police report, your testimony, witnesses' testimony

Defenses: 1. You were contributorily negligent.
2. You were the main cause of the accident.

Consumer Product Purchase

Example: You purchased goods from an individual, store, or business that
- are defective
- do not function or perform as promised
- are not what you ordered

What You Must Prove	*How to Prove It*
1. The date and place of purchase	1. Contract of sale, receipt, your testimony
2. What you bought	2. Contract of sale, receipt
3. That you paid for it	3. Canceled check, receipt
4. (a) The product is defective	4. (a) Your testimony, witnesses, estimates of repair
(b) The product did not perform as promised	(b) Warranties in your contract, written advertisements, statements made to you
(c) The product was not what you ordered	(c) Contract of sale, receipt, your testimony, witnesses

Defenses: 1. The product was used recklessly, carelessly, or in an abnormal manner.

2. Specific promises about the capabilities were never given; the warranties do not apply; there is a disclaimer in the contract.
3. Store or business was never notified of the problem or given a chance to correct it.

Improper Work, Labor, or Services

Example: You pay a person or business to perform work, labor, or services and you:
- do not receive service
- receive inferior workmanship
- receive the wrong service
- you perform work, labor, or services and are not paid

What You Must Prove	How to Prove It
1. The person, company, or business that agreed to perform services	1. Your testimony, contract
2. What work was promised	2. Contract, notes, correspondence, sketches, promotional material
3. What was paid	3. Canceled check, receipt
4. (a) Service was not performed	4. (a) Photographs, your testimony, witnesses
(b) Inferior workmanship	(b) Photographs, your testimony, witnesses, mechanics' estimates of repair
(c) Wrong services performed	(c) Your testimony, witnesses
(d) You performed work competently, for a fee; the defendant accepted the work performed but won't pay	(d) Photographs, your testimony, witnesses, written contract, notes, partial payment by canceled check, receipt

Defenses: 1. Services were performed properly.
2. You were unreasonable (kept changing work plans, etc.).

Wrongful Taking and Bailment

Example: A guest in your home borrows your luggage, you check your coat in a restaurant, store your furs, or order merchandise and the item is
- damaged
- lost
- stolen
- not returned or delivered

What You Must Prove	How to Prove It
1. Time, place, and delivery of the goods to a person, business, or company	1. Contract, receipt, canceled check
2. Description of the property and proof of ownership	2. Bill of sale, your testimony, witnesses
3. Value of property when originally purchased or acquired; current or replacement value	3. Sales receipt, canceled check, appraisal
4. (a) Item is damaged	4. (a) Photographs, estimates of repair, your testimony, witnesses
(b) Item is lost	(b) Your testimony, witnesses, police report, insurance report
(c) Item is stolen	(c) Your testimony, witnesses, police report, insurance report
(d) Item not returned or delivered	(d) Demand letter, your testimony, witnesses
5. Damages	5. Cost or replacement value, canceled check, appraisal, sales receipt

Defenses:
1. Goods were held longer than required.
2. Storage bill was not paid.
3. There is no proof that the goods belong to you or were given to you.

Insurance Policy

Example: You purchase a burglary, accident, fire, or marine insurance policy and the company:
- refuses to pay
- agrees to pay less than you are willing to accept

What You Must Prove	*How to Prove It*
1. A contract of insurance existed at the time the claim was made	1. Insurance policy, insurance binder, representations made by insurance agent
2. The policy was in effect at the time the claim was made	2. Insurance policy, correspondence, premium notice, canceled check
3. You are the owner or beneficiary of the policy	3. Insurance policy, your testimony, witnesses
4. A loss occurred	4. Your testimony, witnesses, photographs, police report
5. You properly notified the company	5. Demand letter (sent certified or registered mail), your testimony, witnesses
6. Damages	6. Your testimony, witnesses, photographs, appraisal

Defenses: 1. There was nonpayment of premium.
2. You failed to perform specified duties as per the policy.
3. You failed to make timely demand as per the policy.
4. Claim is a fraudulent intent to collect.

Goods Sold and Delivered

Example: You sell and deliver goods to a person, business, or company, and those goods are:
- returned for no valid reason
- accepted, used, but not paid for

What You Must Prove	*How to Prove It*
1. Date, time, and person to whom you agreed to sell and deliver goods	1. Contract of sale, memorandum of agreement, your testimony, witnesses
2. The agreement to sell and deliver was made at the request and acceptance of defendant	2. Your testimony, witnesses, agreement, contract of sale, partial payment via canceled check, receipt
3. Date, place, quantity, and description of goods delivered	3. Your testimony, witnesses, delivery receipt
4. Demand for payment	4. Your testimony, witnesses, demand letter
5. Damages	5. Contract price (contract of sale, memorandum letter of agreement), amount of money you lost upon resale (canceled check, receipt)

Defenses: 1. Goods were not of ordered quality.
2. Goods were defective.
3. Goods were shipped late.
4. Goods were never received.

Loan

Example: You lend money to someone and it is not repaid in a timely fashion.

What You Must Prove	*How to Prove It*
1. Date and place you lent the money	1. Your testimony, witnesses
2. Whom you lent the money to	2. Your testimony, witnesses, loan agreement, note of indebtedness
3. Amount of money lent	3. Loan agreement, your testimony, witnesses, note, canceled check

What You Must Prove	*How to Prove It*
4. Amount and time intervals of repayment	4. Loan agreement, your testimony, witnesses
5. Timely demand was made	5. Demand letter (sent certified or registered mail), your testimony, witnesses
6. The amount has not been repaid	6. Your testimony, witnesses

Defenses: 1. Amount of interest charged is usurious.
2. Loan was really a gift.
3. Loan was forgiven.
4. Loan was repaid.

Assault and Battery

Example: You are threatened or injured by a person, or are bitten by a pet.

What You Must Prove	*How to Prove It*
1. Time and place of incident	1. Your testimony, witnesses
2. Facts showing the act was intentional	2. Your testimony, witnesses
3. If a dog bite, show owner, describe dog, place of incident, what you were doing at the time	3. Your testimony, witnesses
4. Injuries you sustained	4. Photographs (preferably color and taken as soon after injury as possible), police report, medical bills, employer's statement of lost wages, letter from doctor showing lost time from work.

Defenses: 1. Incident was provoked or self-defense.
2. Reasonable force was used and justified under the circumstances.

Obtaining Judgment

Some small claims court judges render oral decisions on the spot. Others issue a decision in writing several days after the hearing. This gives them time to weigh the testimony and exhibits. If your opponent failed to attend the hearing, judges usually render a judgment of default immediately after your presentation.

If you win the case, make sure you know how and when payment will be made. Check to see that all of your disbursements—including court costs, filing fees, service of process, and applicable witness fees—are added to the amount of your judgment. Send a copy of the decision by certified mail, return receipt requested, to your opponent, together with a letter requesting payment. Some states require that payment be made to the court, others allow payment to be made directly to you.

Do not hesitate to act if you do not receive the money. First, contact the clerk and file a Petition for Notice to Show Cause. This will be sent to the defendant, ordering him or her to come into court and explain why he or she has not paid. You should also file an Order of Execution with the sheriff's, constable's, or clerk's office in the county where the defendant resides, works, or owns a business. This will enable you to discover where the defendant has assets. The sheriff or other enforcement agent has the power to go out and collect the judgment either by seizing personal property, freezing the defendant's bank accounts, placing a lien on any real estate, or even garnisheeing salary. The clerk of your small claims court will tell you exactly what to do to collect your judgment.

Additional Procedural Points

By bringing suit in small claims court, you usually waive your rights to a trial by jury. However, the defendant can surprise you. Some states allow defendants to move a small claims court case to a higher court and/or obtain a trial by jury. If this occurs, you will need a lawyer to represent you, and his or her services could cost as much as your claim in the dispute.

Some states don't allow losing plaintiffs to appeal. Also, an appeals court will overturn the decision of a small claims court judge only if there is strong proof that the judge was biased or dishonest. This is very difficult to prove. *Prepare your case well the first time, and walk away if you lose.*

ALL ABOUT ARBITRATION

This informal process is used to resolve employment and labor misunderstandings, recover uninsured motorist and no-fault insurance claims, settle disagreements between businesspeople, clarify property distribution clauses in divorce cases, and enforce consumer purchases and contracts.

Arbitrators have broader powers than judges and are not limited by strict rules of evidence. They can hear all relevant testimony when making a decision, including some forms of evidence (hearsay, questionable copies of documents, etc.) that would be excluded in a regular court. Arbitrators have the authority to hear witnesses out of order. Their decisions are legally binding and *unappealable*.

How to Obtain Arbitration

Individuals cannot initiate arbitration hearings merely because they have a dispute that requires legal intervention. In order to obtain a hearing, both parties must agree in writing that the controversy will be submitted to binding arbitration. (Oral agreements to arbitrate disputes are not enforceable.)

The right to proceed to arbitration is usually accomplished by including the following type of clause in an employment contract, lease, loan agreement, or other document:

> Any controversy or claim arising out of or relating to this agreement, or the breach thereof, shall be settled by arbitration in accordance with the Rules of the American Arbitration Association, and judgment upon the award rendered by the arbitrator(s) may be entered in any court having jurisdiction thereof.

By signing an agreement containing such a provision, both parties waive their right to sue in court and agree to submit future disputes to the binding decision of arbitrators.

Hearings can be obtained another way. At any time, the parties are free to sign a document called a "submission agreement." This is usually prepared after a dispute has arisen and the parties agree it is better to arbitrate than face the expense, time delay, and inconvenience of litigation.

To be valid, the submission agreement must disclose the identity of the parties, the nature of the controversy, and the manner of arbitrator selection. For example:

> We, the undersigned parties, hereto submit to arbitration under the Commercial Arbitration Rules of the American Arbitration Association the following controversy (cite briefly). We further agree that the above controversy be submitted to (one) (three) arbitrator(s) selected from the panels of arbitrators of the American Arbitration Association. We further agree that we will faithfully observe this agreement and the Rules and that we will abide by and perform any award.

Both a signed agreement containing an arbitration clause and a submission agreement bind the parties to the arbitration process in most states.

For disputes under $20,000 it costs about $200 to commence a hearing. The figure increases proportionally with the amount at stake—$1,000 for disputes up to $40,000 and $1,400 for disputes up to $80,000.

Advantages and Disadvantages of Arbitration

Expense. Unlike small claims court, you need an attorney for arbitration, but fees are reduced because the average hearing is shorter (typically less than a day) than the average trial. Expensive pretrial procedures, including depositions, interrogatories, and motions, are usually eliminated. Out-of-pocket expenses are reduced because stenographic fees, transcripts, and other items are not required.

Time. Arbitration hearings and final awards are obtained quickly; cases are usually decided in a matter of months, compared to several years in formal litigation.

Privacy. The arbitration hearing is held in a private conference room. Unlike a trial, the hearing cannot be attended by the general public. Thus, unwanted publicity is often avoided.

Expertise. Arbitrators usually have experience in the area of the case. Their knowledge of trade customs helps them identify and understand a problem quicker than a judge or jury.

Finality. Arbitrators, unlike judges, need not give formal reasons for their decisions. Nor are they required to maintain a record of the proceedings. The arbitrator's decision is binding except in a few extraordinary circumstances where arbitrator misconduct, dishonesty, or bias can be proved.

Loss of jury. Some lawyers believe that juries tend to empathize with certain kinds of people. Their view is that salespeople, fired employees, accident victims, destitute wives, and older individuals are better off seeking damages before a jury than a panel of arbitrators. Arbitrators are usually successful lawyers, professionals, and businesspeople, who are not easily swayed by a talented lawyer's style. Their philosophical orientation sometimes leans closer to companies than individuals.

Loss of discovery devices. Some claimants must rely on an adversary's documents and records to prove their case. For example, independent sales agents, songwriters, authors, patent holders, and others often depend on their company's (or licensee's) sales figures and accurate recordkeeping to determine how much commission and royalties are owed. The same is true for minority shareholders who seek a proper assessment of a company's profit picture. These people may be disadvantaged by the arbitration process.

In court, lawyers have ample opportunity to view the private books and records of an adversary before the trial. This is accomplished by pretrial discovery devices such as interrogatories, depositions, and notices to produce documents for inspection and copying. These devices are *not* as readily available to litigants in arbitration. In many instances, records are not viewed until the day of the hearing. This makes it difficult to detect whether they are accurate and complete. And it is often up to the arbitrator's discretion whether to grant an adjournment for the purposes of reviewing such records.

Steps Leading to the Hearing

Commencing the hearing is a relatively simple matter once arbitration has been selected as the method of resolving a dispute. Either you or your lawyer sends a notice, called a "Demand for Arbitration," to the adversary (see Figure 7.2). The notice briefly describes the controversy and specifies the kind of relief sought, including the damages requested. Copies of the demand are sent to the American Arbitration Association (AAA), along with the appropriate administrative fee.

The AAA is most often selected to arbitrate disputes. It is a public service, nonprofit organization that offers dispute settlement services to business executives, individual employees, trade associations, unions, management, consumers, farmers, communities, and all levels of government.

The other party responds to the charges, usually within seven days. It may also allege a counterclaim for damages. Either party can add or change claims in writing until the arbitrator is appointed. At that point, changes can be made only with the arbitrator's consent. After the AAA receives the Demand for Arbitration and reply, an AAA administrator usually supplies the parties with a list of potential arbitrators. The list contains arbitrators' names, occupations, places of employment, and appropriate background information.

Such individuals are usually lawyers, accountants, consultants, and experts in the particular industry or field in which the controversy occurred who have served successfully as arbitrators before. The AAA constantly upgrades their accomplishments and expertise. It also admits new people to its master computer list when such individuals demonstrate a talent to serve as arbitrators or when recommended by other experts in the field; they are included on the list after an interview and analysis and approval of their qualifications. Typically in each case, an AAA administrator will provide the parties with approximately five to ten potential arbitrators randomly selected from the computer (after weeding out for specialty) in each case.

The parties mutually agree to nominees from this list. If the parties do not agree beforehand to the number of arbitrators, the dispute is decided by one arbitrator, unless the AAA determines that three are appropriate. Potential arbitrators are obligated to notify the AAA immediately of any facts likely to affect their impartiality, such as prior dealings with one of the litigants, and disqualify themselves where appropriate.

Once the arbitrator is selected, the AAA administrator schedules a convenient hearing date and location. There is no direct communication between the parties and the arbitrator until the hearing date; all requests, inquiries, and so on are received by the administrator and relayed to the arbitrator. This avoids the appearance of impropriety. The parties are free to request a prehearing conference to exchange documents and resolve certain issues. Typically, however, the parties, administrator, lawyers, and arbitrator meet face-to-face for the first time at the hearing.

The Hearing

Most hearings are conducted in a conference room at an AAA regional office. A stenographer is present, if requested, and the requesting party bears the cost.

The arbitrator introduces the parties and usually asks each side to:

- briefly summarize its version of the dispute
- state what he or she intends to prove at the hearing

The complainant presents his or her case first. Witnesses are called to give testimony (usually under oath). These witnesses are then usually cross-examined by the opposing party's lawyer and may also be questioned by the arbitrator. The complaining party introduces documents, affidavits, and all other supporting materials.

The opposing party then introduces witnesses, documents, and so on. These witnesses are then cross-examined by the opposing party's lawyer and the arbitrator.

Finally, both sides are usually asked to summarize what they believe was proved at the hearing. (Sometimes, before rendering a decision, the arbitrator also requests that both parties submit legal briefs that summarize their positions.) The arbitrator then concludes the hearing.

The Judgment

Arbitrators are generally required to render written decisions within 30 days unless the parties agree to some other time period. When there is more than one arbitrator, a majority decision is required. The arbitrator can make any award that is equitable. He or she can order the losing party to pay additional costs, including AAA filing fees and arbitrator fees.

Legal fees may be awarded if the arbitration clause in the original agreement provided for them.

Arbitrators have no contact with the parties after the hearing. The

AAA administrator notifies the parties of the decision in writing by sending each a copy of the award. The decision in a typical commercial case is brief, with no formal reasons given for a particular award or the basis on which damages were calculated.

It is practically impossible to appeal a losing case. The arbitrator has no power once the case is decided. The matter can only be reviewed by a judge, and judges cannot overturn the award on the grounds of insufficient evidence. The only ways a case can be overturned on review are:

- for arbitrator dishonesty, partiality, or bias
- when no valid agreement existed authorizing the arbitration process
- when an issue was ruled on that the arbitrator was not authorized to decide

In addition, awards are modifiable only if there was a miscalculation of figures or a mistake in the description of the person, property, or thing referred to in the award.

How to Increase Your Chances of Success in Arbitration

Hire the right lawyer. Hire a lawyer who is experienced with the intricacies of the arbitration process.

Prepare for the hearing. It is important that both you and your lawyer carefully prepare for the hearing. Your goal is to submit evidence that will prove your case.

Hire a lawyer who is experienced in the intricacies of the arbitration process.

- Organize the facts: Gather and label all documents you will need at the hearing. Put them in the order they will be presented. Make copies for the arbitrators and your adversary. If some of the documents you need are in the possession of the other party, ask that they be brought to the hearing. In some states, the arbitrator or an attorney of record has the authority to subpoena documents and records.
- Interview witnesses: Be sure that friendly witnesses, if any, will testify on your behalf. If there is the possibility that additional

witnesses may have to appear, alert them to be available. Be sure the witnesses understand the case and the importance of their testimony. Select witnesses who are believable and will not say things at the hearing that will surprise you. Coordinate the witnesses' testimony so that your case is consistent and credible. Prepare them for the rigors of cross-examination. If one of your witnesses requires a translator, make arrangements.

- Consider your opponent's case: Study the controversy from his or her point of view. Anticipate what your opponent will say to defeat your claim and be prepared to refute that evidence.
- Make appropriate arrangements: For example, if it is necessary for the arbitrator to visit a building for an inspection, plan this. The arbitrator must be accompanied by representatives of both sides unless the parties permit the arbitrator to conduct the investigation without them.
- Practice your story: Practicing what you will say will put you at ease and help you organize important facts.
- Act professionally: Show respect for the arbitrators. Listen to their questions and instructions. Never argue with them. If an arbitrator asks you a question while you are speaking, stop immediately. Answer his or her question honestly and to the point. Do not argue with your opponent at the hearing. Interrupt his or her presentation only if absolutely necessary.

What to Do After Obtaining a Judgment

Most losing parties voluntarily comply with the terms of an unfavorable award. However, if you obtain a judgment and your opponent decides not to pay, your lawyer can enforce the judgment in a regular court.

ARGUING YOUR CASE BEFORE A REGULATORY AGENCY

There are thousands of federal and state administrative agencies responsible for enforcing statutory laws. These include state insurance departments, utility commissions, banking departments, and federal agencies including the Federal Trade Commission. The rules and regulations of these agencies spell out in detail what a statutory law means, what it covers, and how it is to be enforced. Many of these agencies require hearings to determine when a person's rights or the regulations have been violated and to define acts or practices that are prohibited by these rules.

Some agencies are supposed to regulate the activity of businesses through hearings, while others compel hearings only after receiving a complaint. Many have the power to assess monetary fines, revoke licenses, or order corrective action such as product recalls. Although agencies are typically empowered to enforce the law by informally negotiating settlements with businesses, some can order settlements and payment to a consumer for damages after a hearing.

Preparation

Each state and agency imposes different requirements for attending and conducting hearings, such as whether a stenographer needs to be present and whether witnesses are required to testify under oath. They also differ on standards of proof required and the effect of the decision (e.g., if you receive a favorable decision, must you relitigate the matter in court before a judge to obtain recompense, or does the agency have the power to help you collect). Thus, before you request a hearing, speak with an employee of the appropriate agency and obtain pertinent information.

- How quickly can you file?
- When will a hearing be convened?
- Will you be required to meet with an investigator before the hearing?
- How long will the hearing last?
- Will you have an opportunity to review your adversary's position and documents in the file before the hearing?
- How can you learn if witnesses will appear on your adversary's behalf to testify against you?
- Should you hire a lawyer to represent you?
- Is a record made of the hearing? In what form?
- Is the agency's decision final and binding or can the determination be appealed internally? If so, how long will the process take?
- Are formal rules of evidence followed at the hearing?
- Can you subpoena witnesses and documents if your adversary fails to produce them?

- Is the preparation and presentation of your claim worth your time and attention or are you better served filing a lawsuit in court?
- What is the specific statute you can read that explains how the hearing is conducted and what will happen after it is concluded?

The Hearing

If you decide to proceed, it is your responsibility to follow the progress of the hearing. Attend the hearing on the date in question. If you cannot be present, speak to an individual responsible for scheduling, explain your reasons, and ask for a more convenient date. Call that individual the day before the old hearing date to confirm that your request has been granted.

When preparing for the hearing, be certain that any friendly witnesses will attend and testify on your behalf. If necessary, ask a representative from the agency to subpoena key disinterested witnesses. Make sure your story or case is organized beforehand. Arrange all evidence so it can be produced readily. Prepare an outline of key points to be discussed and questions to ask each witness, and practice what you will say. This will relax you and help organize the important facts.

Arrive early and advise the scheduling person of your arrival. Bring your evidence and dress in business clothes. The administrative agency judge or authorized representative will conduct the hearing and ask you questions. Keep your answers direct and to the point. Show the judge your evidence. Speak directly to the judge and respond to his or her questions. Refer to him or her as "Your Honor" and do not argue. If you are asked a question while speaking, stop immediately and answer it.

After your opponent has finished testifying, you may have the opportunity to cross-examine the testimony and refute what was said. Do not be intimidated. Ask the judge to intercede on your behalf when you feel your adversary or his attorney is treating you unfairly. Most judges are sympathetic on this issue.

Decisions are not usually obtained immediately after the hearing. You will probably be notified by mail within a couple of weeks.

WHAT YOU SHOULD KNOW ABOUT MEDIATION

In mediation, both parties voluntarily agree to submit their dispute to a neutral third party in the attempt to settle differences without the expense of litigation. (The parties typically split the cost of administration and a mediator, who is paid either hourly or per day.)

Mediation differs from arbitration and formal litigation in one significant respect: Usually the mediator's decision is not final and binding. Indeed, mediators typically do not render a decision; rather, they take the parties down the path to resolving their own dispute. Thus, the parties are free to stop mediation at any time and litigate. Finally, since no one can be forced to use mediation, the procedure will not be effective unless both parties see the advantages of proceeding. Parties usually are not represented by lawyers and do not call witnesses. However, they may bring documents for the mediator to review.

To learn more about mediation or to use this process to resolve a consumer problem, contact your local bar association or nearest American Arbitration Association (AAA) regional office for details. The AAA and private companies in many states have instituted mediation procedures and rules, trained lawyers and volunteers to serve as mediators, and established excellent facilities for a small fee.

Conciliation

You should know the difference between conciliation and mediation. Typically, the third-party conciliator does not meet with both parties at the same time. Rather, he or she speaks to them separately, usually by telephone or mail. Some dispute resolution agencies provide a combination conciliation-mediation service in which the dispute is first handled through conciliation and then, if still unresolved, proceeds to a face-to-face mediation. Typically the conciliator does not spend a great deal of time on the matter. If after a few phone calls the conciliator feels progress can be obtained, a recommendation may be made to bring both parties together in the attempt to resolve the matter amicably. Conciliation is used frequently by public and private agencies, and most conciliators do not charge a fee.

Choosing a Dispute Resolution Method

Many courts are now offering litigants the chance to proceed with mediation and arbitration with trial still available if this "MED-ARB" process fails or is rejected by the parties. While mediation is typically much cheaper and less formal than litigation and the parties are always free to reject the recommendation of the mediator, the outcome of mediation is harder to predict than that of litigation. Also, a party with a strong case may receive less in a compromise than he or she would have obtained in court. Thus, consider your options carefully before agreeing to mediation, arbitration, or litigation.

FIGURE 7.1 Sample Letter of Complaint

Your Name
Address
Date

(Name/Address)

Dear _____,

    On February 6, 1993, I purchased a Sonic Dishwasher, style #1401B, from Bernard's Bargain Store in Tulsa, Oklahoma. It was installed by employees from Bernard's store. The following day the appliance malfunctioned, causing a small electrical fire and damage to my utility room wall. Based on written estimates, the approximate cost of repair to my home totals $972.50. In addition, I am seeking $488.89, which represents the purchase price and/or replacement value of the dishwasher. Demand for this amount was made repeatedly to Mr. Victor Tegeria, general manager of Bernard's Bargain Store, in person on February 9, 1993, and February 12, 1993; by telephone; and by two (2) certified letters dated February 9, 1993, and February 12, 1993. To date, my requests for reimbursement have been ignored.

Sincerely yours,
(Signature)

FIGURE 7.2 Sample Demand for Arbitration

American Arbitration Association

MEDIATION Please consult the Commercial Mediation Rules regarding mediation procedures. If you want the AAA to contact the other party and arrange a mediation, please check this box. ☐

Commercial Arbitration Rules
Demand for Arbitration

Date: _____

To: Name _____
(of the party upon whom the demand is made)

City and State _____ ZIP Code _____
  Telephone(   ) _____ Fax (   ) _____
  Name of Representative _____
  Representative's Address _____
  City and State _____ ZIP Code _____
  Telephone (   ) _____ Fax (   ) _____
    The named claimant, a party to an arbitration agreement contained in a written contract, dated _____, providing for arbitration under the Commercial Arbitration Rules, hereby demands arbitration thereunder.
(Attach arbitration clause or quote it hereunder.)

NATURE OF DISPUTE:

CLAIM OR RELIEF SOUGHT: (amount, if any)

TYPE OF BUSINESS: Claimant _____ Respondent _____

PLEASE TAKE FURTHER NOTICE that, unless written twenty days after service of this Notice of Intention to Arbitrate you apply to stay the arbitration herein pursuant to Article 75 of the New York Civil Practice Law and Rules, you shall thereafter be precluded from objecting that a valid agreement was not made or has not been complied with and from asserting in court the bar of a limitation of time.

HEARING LOCALE REQUESTED: _____
(city and state)

    You are hereby notified that copies of our arbitration agreement and of this demand are being filed with the American Arbitration Association at its office, with the request that it commence the administration of the arbitration. Under the rules, you may file an answering statement within seven days after notice from the administrator.

Signed _____ Title _____
(may be signed by a representative)
Name of Claimant _____
Address (to be used in connection with this case) _____
City and State _____
Telephone ( ) _____
Name of Representative _____
Representative's Address _____
City and State _____ ZIP Code _____
Telephone ( ) _____ Fax ( ) _____

    To institute proceedings, please send three copies of this demand and the arbitration agreement, with the filing fee, as provided for in the rules, to the AAA. Send the original demand to the respondent.

FOR USE IN NEW YORK STATE

FIGURE 7.3 **List of Mediation and Dispute Resolution Organizations**

The following organizations may be able to provide additional information about specific areas of dispute resolution. Many offer catalogs of publications, as well as brochures of general information.

Dispute Resolution

American Arbitration Association
  (AAA)
140 W. 51st Street
New York, N.Y. 10020
(212) 484-1400

American Bar Association
Standing Committee on Dispute
  Resolution
1800 M Street NW, Suite 200
Washington, D.C. 20036
(202) 331-2258

National Academy of Conciliators
7315 Wisconsin Avenue, Suite
  1255N
Bethesda, Md. 20814
(301) 907-7000

National Institute for Dispute
  Resolution
1901 L Street NW, Suite 600
Washington, D.C. 20036
(202) 446-4764

Consumer Information

Consumer Information Center
18 F Street NW, Room G-142
Washington, D.C. 20405
(202) 566-1794

Council of Better Business Bureaus
4200 Wilson Boulevard, Suite 800
Arlington, Va. 22203
(703) 276-0100

Contractor Associations

International Remodeling
  Contractors Association (IRMA)
P.O. Box 17063
West Hartford, Conn. 06117
(203) 233-7442

National Association of Home
  Builders (NAHB)
15th and M Streets NW
Washington, D.C. 20005
(202) 822-0200

National Kitchen and Bath
   Association (NKBA)
124 Main Street
Hackettstown, N.J. 07840
(201) 852-0033

Architects and Designers

American Institute of Architects
   (AIA)
1735 New York Avenue NW
Washington, D.C. 20006
(202) 626-7300

American Society of Interior
   Designers (ASID)
1430 Broadway
New York, NY 10018
(212) 944-9200

Appendix

Useful Addresses

State Licensing Boards for Contractors

Alabama

Requires statewide licensing for commercial contractors. No testing, bond, or insurance required.

    Contact: State Licensing Board for General Contractors
           400 South Union Street, Suite 235
           Montgomery, Ala. 36130
           (205) 242-2839

Alaska

Requires statewide licensing of all contractors. No test required, although pending legislation will soon require testing of general contractors doing residential work. Contractor must be bonded and insured.

    Contact: Department of Commerce and Economic Development
           P.O. Box 110400
           Juneau, Alaska 99811-0400
           (907) 465-2500

Arizona

Requires statewide licensing of all contractors. Requires four years' experience and completion of licensing test. Contractor must be bonded and insured.

Contact: Arizona Registrar of Contractors
800 West Washington, 6th Floor
Phoenix, Ariz. 85007
(602) 542-1525

Arkansas

Requires license for nonresidential contractors. Applicants must show experience, pass a licensing test, and post a bond. Insurance is optional. Residential construction is not state regulated.

Contact: Contractors Licensing Board
621 East Capitol
Little Rock, Ark. 72202
(501) 372-4661

California

Requires statewide licensing for all contractors. Requires four years' verified experience and completion of licensing test. Requires contractor have both bond and insurance.

Contact: Contractors State Licensing Board
9835 Goethe Road
Sacramento, Calif. 95827
(916) 366-5153 or (800) 321-2752

Colorado

No statewide licensing of building contractors.

Contact: Building department in city or county where construction is to be performed.

Connecticut

Requires statewide registration of home-improvement contractors. No experience or testing required. Contractors must carry worker's compensation insurance but no liability insurance required. No bonding required; contractors pay annually into a home-improvement warranty fund.

Contact: Department of Consumer Protection
Occupational Licensing Division
165 Capital Avenue
Hartford, Conn. 06106
(203) 566-2822

Delaware
Requires statewide licensing for all contractors. Some licenses also issued by cities and counties. No experience or testing required. Contractors must be bonded and insured.

Contact: Division of Revenue
P.O. Box 2340
Wilmington, Del. 19899-2340
(302) 577-5800 or (302) 577-3369

Florida
Requires statewide licensing of all contractors. Requires experience and completion of test. Requires contractor have bond and insurance.

Contact: Construction Industry Licensing Board
P.O. Box 2
Jacksonville, Fla. 32201
(904) 359-6310

Georgia
Requires statewide licensing of plumbing, electrical, heating and air-conditioning, alarm, and utility contractors. Experience and testing required. No insurance or bond required.

Contact: Georgia Construction Industry Licensing Board
166 Pryor Street, SW
Atlanta, Ga. 30303
(404) 656-3939
City or county where construction work is to be performed.

Hawaii
Requires statewide licensing for all types of contractors. Requires successful completion of licensing test. Bonding required for some classifications of contractors. Requires worker's compensation insurance; other insurance optional.

Contact: Department of Commerce and Consumer Affairs
Board of Contractors
1010 Richards Street
Honolulu, Hawaii 96813
(808) 586-2700

Idaho

Requires statewide license for public works contractors only. Some cities also license residential contractors. Requires open-book license test; no bond or insurance.

    Contact: Contractors Licensing Board
             500 South 10th Street, Suite 105
             Boise, Idaho 83720-7000
             (208) 334-2966
             City or county where construction work is to be performed.

Illinois

No statewide licensing of building contractors.

    Contact: Building department in city or county where construction is to be performed.

Indiana

No statewide licensing of building contractors.

    Contact: Building department in city or county where construction is to be performed.

Iowa

Requires statewide licensing of all contractors. No testing or experience required. Contractor must be insured and bonded.

    Contact: Division of Labor
             1000 East Grand Avenue
             Des Moines, Iowa 50319
             (515) 281-3606

Kansas

No statewide licensing of building contractors.

    Contact: Building department in city or county where construction is to be performed.

Kentucky

Requires statewide licensing for plumbing, sprinkler, and boiler contractors only. Requires completion of licensing test. Insurance required; no bond.

    Contact: Department of Housing, Buildings, and Construction
             Division of Building Codes Enforcement
             1047 U.S. 127 South, The 127 Building
             Frankfort, Ky. 40601-4337
             (502) 564-8090

Louisiana

Requires contractors be licensed for construction projects valued at $50,000 or more. Requires asbestos removal and hazardous waste contractors be licensed. Licensing test is required for all of these categories. No experience required. Bonding and insurance are optional.

Contact: Department of Commerce
Contractor's Licensing Board
P.O. Box 14419
Baton Rouge, La. 70898-4419
(504) 765-2301

Maine

Requires statewide licensing for plumbers and electricians.

Contact: Professional and Financial Regulation Department
License and Enforcement Division
State House 35
Augusta, Maine 04333
(207) 582-8723

Maryland

Requires statewide licensing of home-improvement contractors. Licensing test required; worker's compensation insurance required; bonding and other insurance optional.

Contact: Department of Licensing and Regulation
Home Improvement Commission
501 St. Paul Place
Baltimore, Md. 21202
(301) 333-8120

Also requires that contractors engaged in new residential construction be licensed, which is essentially a revenue license. No test required. Requires worker's compensation insurance; bonding optional.

Contact: Department of Revenue
301 West Preston Street, Room 404
Baltimore, Md. 21201
(301) 225-1550

Massachusetts

Requires statewide licensing for all contractors. Contractor must be at least eighteen years old, show three years' verified experience, and pass a licensing test. Bond and insurance are optional.

Contact: Commonwealth of Massachusetts
Registration Division, Room 1301
1 Ashburn Place
Boston, Mass. 02108
(617) 727-3200

Michigan

Requires statewide licensing for residential and commercial construction and remodeling. Requires licensing test. No insurance or bond required.

Contact: Department of Licensing and Registration
Builders Unit
P.O. Box 30245, 611 West Ottawa
Lansing, Mich. 48909
(517) 373-0678

Minnesota

No statewide licensing of building contractors.

Contact: Building department in city or county where construction work is to be performed.

Mississippi

Requires statewide licensing for contractors doing public work valued at over $100,000 or private work valued at over $50,000. Requires licensing test. No bond or insurance required.

Contact: Mississippi State Contractor's Board
2001 Airport Road, Suite 101
Jackson, Miss. 39208
(601) 354-6161

Missouri

No statewide licensing of building contractors.

Contact: Building department in city or county where construction work is to be performed.

Montana

Requires licensing for electrical, plumbing, and public works contractors only. No test, bond, or insurance required.

Contact: Montana Department of Commerce
Building Codes Bureau
Capitol Station
Helena, Mont. 59620
(406) 444-3933

Nebraska
No statewide licensing of building contractors.
Contact: Building department in city or county where construction work is to be performed.

Nevada
Requires statewide licensing for all contractors. Requires four years' verified experience and completion of licensing test. Requires contractor have both bond and insurance.
Contact: State Contractor's Board
1800 Industrial Road
Las Vegas, Nev. 89158
(702) 486-3500

State Contractor's Board
70 Linden Street
Reno, Nev. 89502
(702) 688-1141 or 688-1144

New Hampshire
No statewide licensing of building contractors.
Contact: Building department in city or county where construction work is to be performed.

New Jersey
Requires statewide registration for new-construction contractors. Requires insurance and bond covering a 10-year limited warranty on the home. No requirements for remodeling contractors.
Contact: Bureau of Home Owner Protection
New Jersey Department of Community Affairs
CN 805
Trenton, N.J. 08625-0805
(609) 530-6357

New Mexico
Requires statewide licensing of all contractors. Requires two to four years' experience and completion of a licensing test. Contractors required by state labor department to be insured. Bond is one option of proof of financial responsibility.

Contact: Regulation and Licensing Department
Construction Industries Division
P.O. Box 25101
Santa Fe, N.M. 87504
(505) 827-7030 or 827-7059

New York
No statewide licensing of building contractors.
Contact: Building department in city or county where construction work is
to be performed.

North Carolina
Requires statewide licensing for contractors. No experience required but licensing test must be passed. No bond or insurance required.
Contact: North Carolina Licensing Board for General Contractors
P.O. Box 17187
Raleigh, N.C. 27619
(919) 571-4183

North Dakota
Requires statewide licensing of all contractors. No experience or testing required. Requires worker's compensation and liability insurance; contractor must be bonded.
Contact: Secretary of State
Capitol Building, 1st Floor
600 East Boulevard Avenue
Bismarck, N.D. 58505-0500
(701) 224-3665

Ohio
No statewide licensing of building contractors.
Contact: Building department in city or county where construction work is
to be performed.

Oklahoma
Requires statewide licensing for plumbing, electrical, heating and air-conditioning, and alarm contractors only. Requires completion of a test. Requires insurance and bond.
Contact: Oklahoma Department of Health
1000 Northeast 10th
Oklahoma City, Okla. 73152
(405) 271-5600

Oregon

Requires statewide licensing of all contractors. No experience or testing required. Requires worker's compensation and liability insurance; contractor must be bonded.

Contact: Construction Contractor's Board
700 Summer Street, NE
Salem, Oreg. 97310
(503) 378-4621

Pennsylvania

No statewide licensing of building contractors.

Contact: Building department in city or county where construction work is to be performed.

Rhode Island

Requires statewide registration of contractors. No experience or test required. Contractor must carry insurance; no bond.

Contact: Department of Labor
Contractor Registration
220 Elmwood Avenue
Providence, R.I. 02907
(401) 457-1860

South Carolina

Requires statewide licensing of commercial, public works, electrical, plumbing, and heating contractors only. Experience and testing required; contractor must be bonded and insured.

Contact: South Carolina Board of Contractors
P.O. Box 5737
Columbia, S.C. 29250
(803) 734-8954

South Dakota

Requires statewide licensing for plumbing and electrical contractors. Must verify experience and pass licensing test.

Contact: Department of Commerce and Regulation
Professional and Occupational Licensing
500 East Capitol Avenue
Pierre, S.D. 57501-5070
(605) 773-3177

Tennessee

Requires statewide licensing for contractors doing work valued at $25,000 or more. Requires completion of test. No bond or insurance required.

    Contact: Contractor's Licensing Board
              500 James Robertson Parkway, Suite 110
              Nashville, Tenn. 37219
              (615) 741-8307

Texas

No statewide licensing of building contractors.

    Contact: Building department in city or county where construction work is to be performed.

Utah

Requires statewide licensing of all contractors. Requires four years' verified experience and completion of licensing test. Contractors must be insured; no bond required.

    Contact: Division of Occupational and Professional Licensing
              P.O. Box 45805
              Salt Lake City, Utah 84145-0805
              (801) 530-6514

Vermont

No statewide licensing of building contractors.

    Contact: Building department in city or county where construction work is to be performed.

Virginia

Requires statewide testing and licensing for all contractors. Requires insurance; may require bond at local level.

    Contact: Contractor's Board
              3600 West Broad Street
              Richmond, Va. 23230
              (804) 367-8511

Washington

Requires statewide licensing of all contractors. No licensing test required. Contractors must be bonded and insured.

Contact: Department of Labor and Industries
Contractor's Registration
P.O. Box 44450, 805 Plum Street
Olympia, Wash. 98504
(206) 586-6085

West Virginia
No statewide licensing of building contractors.
Contact: Building department in city or county where construction work is
to be performed.

Wisconsin
No statewide licensing of building contractors.
Contact: Building department in city or county where construction work is
to be performed.

Wyoming
No statewide licensing of building contractors.
Contact: Building department in city or county where construction work is
to be performed.

Appraisers' Associations

Accredited Gemologists Association
3 Ross Commons
Ross, Calif. 94957
(415) 461-5900

American Diamond Industry
   Association
71 West 47th Street, Suite 705
New York, N.Y. 10036
(212) 575-0525

American Society of Appraisers
535 Herndon Parkway
Herndon, Va. 22070
(703) 478-2228

Antique Appraisal Association of
   America
11361 Garden Grove Boulevard
Garden Grove, Calif. 92643
(714) 530-7090

Appraisers Association of America
60 East 42d Street, Suite 2505
New York, N.Y. 10165
(212) 867-9775

International Society of Appraisers
4805 West Berkley Lane
Hoffman Estates, Ill. 60194

International Society of Fine Arts
   Appraisers, Ltd.
P.O. Box 280
River Forest, Ill. 60305

Mid-Am Antique Appraisers
   Association
P.O. Box 9681
Springfield, Mo. 65801
(417) 865-7269

National Association of Jewelry
  Appraisers
P.O. Box 6558
Annapolis, Md. 21401-0558
(301) 261-8270

Registered Appraisers of Florida, Inc.
P.O. Box 15797
Sarasota, Fla. 33579

Regional Offices of the American Arbitration Association

333 East Osborn, Suite 310
Phoenix, Ariz. 85012-2803
(602) 234-0950

2601 Main Street, Suite 240
Irvine, Calif. 92714-6220
(714) 474-5090

443 Shatto Place
Los Angeles, Calif. 90020-1781
(213) 383-6516

525 C Street, Suite 400
San Diego, Calif. 92101-5278
(619) 239-3051

417 Montgomery Street
San Francisco, Calif. 94104-1113
(415) 981-3901

1660 Lincoln Street, Suite 2150
Denver, Colo. 80264-2101
(303) 831-0823

111 Founders Plaza, 17th Floor
East Hartford, Conn. 06108
(203) 289-3993

1150 Connecticut Avenue, NW, 6th
  Floor
Washington, D.C. 20036-4104
(202) 296-8510

99 Southeast 5th Street, Suite 200
Miami, Fla. 33131-2501
(305) 358-7777

201 East Pine Street, Suite 800
Orlando, Fla. 32801-2742
(407) 648-1185

1360 Peachtree Street, NE, Suite 270
Atlanta, Ga. 30309-3598
(404) 872-3022

810 Richards Street, Suite 641
Honolulu, Hawaii 96813-4728
(808) 531-0541

225 North Michigan Avenue, Suite 2527
Chicago, Ill. 60601
(312) 616-6560

650 Poydras Street, Suite 1535
New Orleans, La. 70130-6101
(504) 522-8781

133 Federal Street
Boston, Mass. 02110-1703
(617) 451-6600

10 Oak Hollow Street, Suite 170
Southfield, Mich. 48034-7405
(313) 352-5500

514 Nicollet Avenue, Suite 670
Minneapolis, Minn. 55402-1092
(612) 332-6545

1101 Walnut Street, Suite 903
Kansas City, Mo. 64106-2110
(816) 221-6401

1 Mercantile Center, Suite 2512
St. Louis, Mo. 63101-1614
(314) 621-7175

265 Davidson Avenue, Suite 140
Somerset, N.J. 08873-4120
(908) 560-9560

666 Old Country Road, Suite 603
Garden City, N.Y. 11530-2004
(516) 222-1660

140 West 51st Street
New York, N.Y. 10020-1203
(212) 484-4000

205 South Salina Street
Syracuse, N.Y. 13202-1376
(315) 472-5483

34 South Broadway
White Plains, N.Y. 10601-4485
(914) 946-1119

428 East 4th Street, Suite 300
Charlotte, N.C. 28202
(704) 347-0200

441 Vine Street, Suite 3308
Cincinnati, Ohio 45202-2973
(513) 241-8434

17900 Jefferson Park West, Suite 101
Middleburgh Heights, Ohio 44130
(216) 891-4741

230 South Broad Street, 6th Floor
Philadelphia, Pa. 19102
(215) 732-5260

419 Gateway 4
Pittsburgh, Pa. 15222-1207
(412) 261-3617

221 4th Avenue North, 2nd Floor
Nashville, Tenn. 37219-2111
(615) 256-5857

13455 Noel Road, Suite 1440
Dallas, Tex. 75240-6620
(214) 702-8222

1001 Fannin Street, Suite 1005
Houston, Tex. 77002-6708
(713) 739-1302

645 South 200 East, Suite 203
Salt Lake City, Utah 84111-3834
(801) 531-9748

1325 4th Avenue, Suite 14
Seattle, Wash. 98101-2511
(206) 622-6435

Where to Complain

(Consult your Yellow Pages for the local address.)

Accountants	State Education Department
Airlines	United States Department of Transportation, Federal Aviation Authority
Animals	Animal Affairs Bureau
Architects	State Education Department
Automobiles	National Highway Traffic Safety Administration
Automobile Rentals	Department of Consumer Affairs
Automobile Repairs	Department of Motor Vehicles, Better Business Bureau, Department of Consumer Affairs
Banks	United States Comptroller of the Currency, Federal Reserve Bank, state banking department
Charities	State Attorney General
Chiropractors	State Education Department
Computers	Department of Consumer Affairs
Dentists	State Education Department

Discrimination	Division of Human Rights, Equal Employment Opportunity Commission
Doctors	State Health Department, American Medical Association
Dry Cleaners	Better Business Bureau, Department of Consumer Affairs
Food	Food and Drug Administration, Department of Agriculture, State Department of Agriculture and Markets, Department of Consumer Affairs
Funerals	State Health Department, Federal Trade Commission
Furniture	Department of Consumer Affairs, Better Business Bureau
Garbage	Department of Sanitation
Home Improvements	Department of Consumer Affairs
Insurance	State Insurance Department, Attorney General's Office
Lawyers	Legal Referral Department of Lawyers Disciplinary Committee, American Bar Association
Mail-order Sales	Department of Consumer Affairs, Federal Trade Commission, Postal Service
Moving and Storage	Interstate Commerce Commission, Department of Transportation, Department of Consumer Affairs
Noise	Department of Environmental Protection
Notaries	State Education Department
Nursing Homes	Department of Health, Attorney General's Office
Pharmacists	State Education Department
Police Misconduct	Civilian Complaint Review Board
Potholes	Department of Transportation
Real Estate Brokers	State Education Department, Department of State
Repairs	Department of Consumer Affairs
Restaurants	Department of Health

Social Workers	State Education Department
Stockbrokers	Securities and Exchange Commission
Taxis	Taxi and Limousine Commission
Veterinarians	State Education Department
Utilities	Public Service Commission
Water	Department of Health

Offices of State Attorneys General

Alabama
Attorney General
11 South Union Street
Montgomery, Ala. 36130
(205) 242-7300

Alaska
Attorney General
Department of Law
120 4th Street
Juneau, Alaska 99801
(907) 465-3600

Arizona
Attorney General
1275 West Washington
Phoenix, Ariz. 85007
(602) 542-4266

Arkansas
Attorney General
Office of the Attorney General

323 Center, Suite 200
Little Rock, Ark. 72201
(501) 682-2007

California
Attorney General
Office of the Attorney General
Department of Justice
1515 K Street, Law Library
Sacramento, Calif. 95814
(916) 324-5437

Colorado
Attorney General
Department of Law
110 16th Street, 10th Floor
Denver, Colo. 80202
(303) 620-4500

Connecticut
Attorney General
55 Elm Street
Hartford, Conn. 06106
(203) 566-2026

Delaware
Attorney General
Carvel State Office Building
820 North French Street
Wilmington, Del. 19801
(302) 571-2500

Florida
Attorney General
Department of Legal Affairs
The Capitol
Tallahassee, Fla. 32399
(904) 487-1963

Georgia
Attorney General
State Law Department
132 State Judicial Building
Atlanta, Ga. 30334
(404) 656-4585

Hawaii
Attorney General
Department of the Attorney General
425 Queen Street
Honolulu, Hawaii 96813
(808) 586-1282

Idaho
Attorney General
Office of the Attorney General
State Capitol
Boise, Idaho 83720
(208) 334-2424

Illinois
Attorney General
500 South Second Street
Springfield, Ill. 62706
(217) 782-1090

Indiana
Attorney General
219 State House
Indianapolis, Ind. 46204
(317) 232-6201

Iowa
Attorney General
Hoover State Office Building
Des Moines, Iowa 50319
(515) 281-8373

Kansas
Attorney General
301 West Tenth, Judicial Center
Topeka, Kans. 66612
(913) 296-2215

Kentucky
Attorney General
State Capitol, Room 116
Frankfort, Ky. 40601
(502) 564-7600

Louisiana
Attorney General
Department of Justice
P.O. Box 94005
Baton Rouge, La. 70804
(504) 342-7013

Maine
Attorney General
Department of the Attorney General
State House Station # 6
Augusta, Maine 04333
(207) 289-3661

Maryland
Attorney General
200 Saint Paul Place
Baltimore, Md. 21202
(301) 576-6300

Massachusetts
Attorney General
1 Ashburton Place
Boston, Mass. 02108
(617) 727-3688

Michigan
Attorney General
525 West Ottawa, Law Building
Lansing, Mich. 48913
(517) 373-1110

Minnesota
Attorney General
102 State Capitol
St. Paul, Minn. 55155
(612) 297-4272

Mississippi
Attorney General
P.O. Box 220
Jackson, Miss. 39205
(601) 359-3680

Missouri
Attorney General
Supreme Court Building
P.O. Box 899
Jefferson City, Mo. 65102
(314) 751-3221

Montana
Attorney General
Department of Justice
215 North Sanders Street
Helena, Mont. 59620
(406) 444-2026

Nebraska
Attorney General
State Capitol, Room 2115
P.O. Box 94906
Lincoln, Nebr. 68509
(402) 471-2682

Nevada
Attorney General
Heroes Memorial Building
Capitol Complex
Carson City, Nev. 89710
(702) 687-4170

New Hampshire
Attorney General
State House Annex, Room 208
25 Capitol Street
Concord, N.H. 03301
(603) 271-3658

New Jersey
Attorney General
Office of the Attorney General
Department of Law and Public Safety
Hughes Justice Complex, CN 081
Trenton, N.J. 08625
(609) 292-8740

New Mexico
Attorney General
Bataan Memorial Building
P.O. Box 1508
Santa Fe, N.M. 87501
(505) 827-6000

New York
Attorney General
Department of Law
State Capitol
Albany, N.Y. 12224
(518) 474-7330

North Carolina
Attorney General
Department of Justice
2 East Morgan Street
Raleigh, N.C. 27601
(919) 733-3377

North Dakota
Attorney General
State Capitol, 1st Floor
600 East Boulevard
Bismarck, N.D. 58505
(701) 224-2210

Ohio
Attorney General
30 East Broad Street, 17th Floor
Columbus, Ohio 43266
(614) 466-3376

Oklahoma
Attorney General
112 State Capitol
Oklahoma City, Okla. 73105
(405) 521-3921

Oregon
Attorney General
Department of Justice
100 State Office Building
Salem, Oreg. 97310
(503) 378-6002

Pennsylvania
Attorney General
Strawberry Square, 16th Floor
Harrisburg, Pa. 17120
(717) 787-3391

Rhode Island
Attorney General
72 Pine Street
Providence, R.I. 02903
(401) 274-4400

South Carolina
Attorney General
Dennis Building
P.O. Box 11549
Columbia, S.C. 29211
(803) 734-3970

South Dakota
Attorney General
State Capitol, 1st Floor
Pierre, S.D. 57501
(605) 773-3215

Tennessee
Attorney General
450 James Robertson Parkway
Nashville, Tenn. 37243
(615) 741-6474

Texas
Attorney General
Capitol Station
P.O. Box 12548
Austin, Tex. 78711
(512) 463-2100

Utah
Attorney General
236 State Capitol
Salt Lake City, Utah 84114
(801) 538-1326

Vermont
Attorney General
Pavilion Office Building
109 State Street
Montpelier, Vt. 05602
(802) 828-3171

Virginia
Attorney General
Office of the Attorney General
101 North Eighth Street, 5th Floor
Richmond, Va. 23219
(804) 786-2071

Washington
Attorney General
Highway Licenses Bldg.
M/S: PB-71
Olympia, Wash. 98504
(206) 753-2550

West Virginia
Attorney General
Building 1, Room E-26
State Capitol Complex
Charleston, W.V. 25305
(304) 348-2021

Wisconsin
Attorney General
Department of Justice
114 East State Capitol
P.O. Box 7857
Madison, Wis. 53707
(608) 266-1221

Wyoming
Attorney General
State Capitol
Cheyenne, Wyo. 82002
(307) 777-7810

District of Columbia
Corporation Counsel
Office of the Corporation Counsel
1350 Pennsylvania, NW, Room 329
Washington, D.C. 20004
(202) 727-6248

American Samoa
Attorney General
Legal Affairs
Office of the Attorney General
Pago Pago, Amer. Samoa 96799
(684) 633-4163

Guam
Attorney General
Office of the Attorney General
238 Archbishop Flores Street, Suite 701
Agana, Guam 96910
(671) 472-6841

Northern Mariana Islands
Attorney General
Office of the Attorney General
Capitol Hill
Administration Building, 2nd Floor
Saipan, M.P. 96950
(670) 322-4311

Puerto Rico
Secretary
Department of Justice
P.O. Box 192
San Juan, P.R. 00904
(809) 721-2924

U.S. Virgin Islands
Attorney General
Department of Justice
GERS Building, Second Floor
St. Thomas, V.I. 00802
(809) 774-5666

Federal Trade Commission Regional Offices

Atlanta—Alabama, Florida, Georgia, Mississippi, North Carolina, South Carolina, Tennessee, Virginia

Room 1000, 1718 Peachtree Street, NW, Atlanta, Ga. 30367

Boston—Connecticut, Maine, Massachusetts, New Hampshire, Rhode Island, Vermont

Room 1184, 10 Causeway Street, Boston, Mass. 02222-1073

Chicago—Illinois, Indiana, Iowa, Kentucky, Minnesota, Missouri, Wisconsin

Suite 1437, 55 East Monroe Street, Chicago, Ill. 60603

Cleveland—Delaware, Maryland, Michigan, Ohio, Pennsylvania, West Virginia

Suite 520-A, 668 Euclid Avenue, Cleveland, Ohio 44114

Dallas—Arkansas, Louisiana, New Mexico, Oklahoma, Texas

Suite 500, 100 North Central Expressway, Dallas, Tex. 75201

Denver—Colorado, Kansas, Montana, Nebraska, North Dakota, South Dakota, Utah, Wyoming

Suite 2900, 1405 Curtis Street, Denver, Colo. 80202-2393

Los Angeles—Arizona, southern California

Suite 13209, 11000 Wilshire Boulevard, Los Angeles, Calif. 90024

New York—New Jersey, New York

Suite 13, 150 William Street, New York, N.Y. 10038

San Francisco—Northern California, Hawaii, Nevada

Suite 570, 901 Market Street, San Francisco, Calif. 94103

Seattle—Alaska, Idaho, Oregon, Washington

2806 Federal Building, 915 2d Avenue, Seattle, Wash. 98174

Glossary

You can reduce the chances of being exploited in your personal business dealings by understanding the meaning of the words in this glossary. In addition, you will be able to communicate better with your lawyer because these terms are commonly used in legal proceedings.

Abuse of process   A cause of action that arises when one party willfully misuses the legal process to injure another

Accord and satisfaction   An agreement between two parties to settle a dispute by compromise

Action in accounting   A type of lawsuit where one party seeks a determination of the amount of money owed by another

Admissible   Capable of being introduced in court as evidence

Advance   A sum of money that is usually applied against money to be earned; sometimes referred to as "draw"

Affidavit   A written statement signed under oath

Allegations   Charges one party expects to prove in a lawsuit

Answer   The defendant's reply to the plaintiff's charges in a civil lawsuit

Appeal   A proceeding whereby the losing party in a lawsuit applies to a higher court to determine the correctness of that decision

Arbitration   A proceeding where both sides submit their dispute to the binding decision of arbitrators rather than judges

Assault and battery   A harmful, offensive, unpermitted touching of one person by another

Assignment   The transfer of a right or interest by one party to another

Attorney in fact   A person appointed by another to transact business on his or her behalf; the person does not have to be a lawyer

Award   A decision made by a judicial body to compensate the winning party for losses or injuries caused by another

Bail bondsman   A person who posts money for a fee to free an incarcerated individual

Bailment   A legal relationship created when one person delivers property to another

Bill of particulars   A document used in a lawsuit that adds information contained in the plaintiff's complaint

Bonus   A sum of money paid by an employer to an employee

Breach of contract   The unjustified failure of a party to perform a duty or obligation specified in a contract

Breach of warranty   A legal cause of action often arising when a seller makes false representations regarding his or her product or service

Burden of proof   The responsibility for a party in a lawsuit to provide sufficient evidence to prove its claims

Business deduction   A legitimate expense that can be used to decrease the amount of reportable income subject to tax

Business slander   A legal wrong committed when a party orally makes false statements that impugn the business reputation of another (e.g., imply that the person is dishonest, incompetent, or financially unreliable)

Calendar   A list of cases to be heard each day in court

Cause of action   Legal theories that the plaintiff alleges in a complaint to recover damages from his or her opponent

Caveat emptor   A Latin expression frequently applied to consumer transactions; translated as "Let the buyer beware"

Certificate of incorporation   A document creating a corporation

Check   A negotiable instrument; the depositor's written order requesting his or her bank to pay a definite sum of money to a named individual or business

Civil court   Generally, any court that presides over noncriminal matters

Claims court   A particular court that hears tax disputes

Clerk of the court   A person who determines whether court papers are properly filed and court procedures followed

Common carrier   An entity that transports persons and property for a fee

Common law   Law that evolves from reported case decisions that are relied upon for their precedential value

Compensatory damages   A sum of money awarded to a party by a court or jury representing the actual harm or loss suffered

Complaint   A legal document that starts a lawsuit; the complaint alleges facts and causes of action that the plaintiff relies upon to collect damages

Computer consultant   A person hired to match his or her client's needs with appropriate computer hardware and software equipment

Conflict of interest   The ethical inability of a lawyer to represent a client because of competing loyalties

Consideration   An essential element of an enforceable contract; something of value given or promised by one party in exchange for an act or promise of another

Contempt   A legal sanction imposed when a rule or order of a judicial body is disobeyed

Contingency fee   A type of fee arrangement where the lawyer is paid a percentage of the money recovered

Continuance   The postponement of a legal proceeding to another date

Contract   An enforceable agreement, either in writing, oral, or implied

Contract modification   The alteration of contract terms

Counterclaim   A claim asserted by the defendant in a lawsuit

Covenant   A promise

Credibility   The believability of a witness in the minds of a judge or jury

Creditor   The party to whom money is owed

Cross-examination   The questioning of a witness by the opposing lawyer

Damages   An award, usually money, given to the winning party in a lawsuit as compensation for the wrongful acts of another

Debtor   The party who owes money

Decision   The determination of a case or matter by a judicial body

Deductible premium   The unrecoverable portion of insurance proceeds

Defamation   An oral or written statement communicated to a third party that impugns a person's reputation in the community

Default judgment   An award rendered after one party fails to appear in a lawsuit

Defendant   The person or business who is sued in a lawsuit

Defense   The defendant's justification for relieving himself or herself of fault

Definite term of employment   Employment for a fixed period of time

Deposition   A pretrial proceeding where one party is questioned, usually under oath, by the opposing party's lawyer

Disclaimer   A clause in a sales, service, or other contract that attempts to limit or exonerate one party from liability in the event of a lawsuit

Discovery   A general term used to describe several pretrial devices (e.g., depositions, interrogatories, etc.) that enable lawyers to elicit information from the opposing side

District court   A particular court that hears tax disputes

Dual capacity   A legal theory used to circumvent worker's compensation laws and allow an injured employee to sue his employer directly in court

Due process   Constitutional protections that guarantee that a person's life, liberty, or property cannot be taken away without the opportunity to be heard in a judicial proceeding

Duress   Unlawful threats, pressure, or force that induce a person to act contrary to his or her intentions; duress, if proved, will allow a party to disavow a contract

Employee A person who works and is subject to an employer's scope, direction, and control

Employment at will Employment that does not provide an employee with job security, since the person can be fired on a moment's notice with or without cause

Employment discrimination Conduct directed at employees and job applicants that is prohibited by law

Equity Fairness; the term is usually applied when a judicial body awards a suitable remedy other than money to a party (e.g., an injunction)

Escrow account A separate fund where lawyers are obligated to deposit money received from or on behalf of a client

Evidence Information in the form of oral testimony, exhibits, affidavits, and so on, used to prove a party's claim

Examination before trial A pretrial legal device; also called a "deposition"

Exempt from execution Property or assets that cannot be seized to satisfy a judgment

Exhibits Tangible evidence used to prove a party's claims

Exit agreements Agreements sometimes signed between employers and employees upon termination or resignation of an employee's services

False arrest The unlawful detention of one person by another who claims to have sufficient legal authority

False imprisonment The unlawful detention of a person who is held against his or her will without authority or justification

Field examination An audit conducted by IRS agents at a taxpayer's home or business

Filing fee Money paid to start a lawsuit

Financial statement A document usually prepared by an accountant that reflects a business's assets, liabilities, and financial condition

Flat fee A sum of money paid to a lawyer as compensation for his or her services

Flat fee plus time A form of payment where a lawyer receives one sum for his or her services, and then receives additional money that is calculated on an hourly basis

Fraud   False statements of an existing fact relied upon and causing damages to the defrauded party

General denial   A reply contained in the defendant's answer

Guaranty   A contract where one party agrees to answer for or satisfy the debt of another

Hardware   A computer unit

Hearsay evidence   Unsubstantiated evidence that is often excluded by a court

Hourly fee   Money paid to a lawyer for his or her services that is computed on an hourly basis

Independent contractor   A worker not subject to an employer's scope, direction, and control, and who pays his or her own social security, withholding tax, and unemployment insurance

Infliction of emotional distress   A legal cause of action where one party seeks to recover damages for mental pain and suffering caused by another

Injunction   A court order restraining one party from doing or refusing to do an act

Interrogatories   A pretrial device used to elicit information; written questions are sent to an opponent to be answered under oath

Invasion of privacy   The violation of a person's constitutionally protected right to privacy

Judgment   A verdict rendered by a judicial body; if money is awarded, the winning party is called the "judgment creditor," and the losing party is called the "judgment debtor"

Jurisdiction   The authority of a court to hear a particular matter

Legal duty   The responsibility of a party to perform a certain act

Letter of agreement   An enforceable contract in the form of a letter

Letter of protest   A letter sent to document a party's dissatisfaction

Liable   Legally in the wrong

Lien   A claim asserted against another party's property to satisfy a judgment

Lifetime contract   An employment agreement of an infinite duration that is often unenforceable

Limited partnership   A type of partnership with general partners and limited partners. Limited partners are liable only to the extent of money invested in the partnership

Liquidated damages   An amount of money agreed upon in advance by parties to a contract to be paid in the event of a breach or dispute

Malicious interference with contract rights   A legal cause of action where one party seeks to recover damages against another who induces or causes a party to terminate a valid contract

Malicious prosecution   A legal cause of action where one party seeks to recover damages after another party instigates or institutes a phony judicial proceeding (usually criminal) that is dismissed

Malpractice   The failure of a professional to render work, labor, services, or skill of suitable competence

Mediation   A voluntary dispute resolution process where both sides attempt to settle their differences without resorting to formal litigation

Medical malpractice   A legal cause of action where one party seeks to recover damages against a doctor for his or her failure to render services or skill of suitable competence

Misappropriation   The unlawful taking of another party's personal property

Misrepresentation   A legal cause of action that arises when one party makes untrue statements of fact that induce another party to act and be damaged as a result

Mitigation of damages   A legal principle that requires a party seeking damages to make reasonable efforts to reduce damages as much as possible; for example, to seek new employment after being unfairly discharged

Motion   A written request made to a court by one party during a lawsuit

Negligence   A party's failure to exercise a sufficient degree of care owed to another by law

No-fault insurance   A system of compensation whereby a victim injured in an auto accident is paid regardless of fault

Nominal damages   A small sum of money awarded by a court

Noncompetition clause   A restrictive provision in a contract

Notary public   A person authorized under state law to administer an oath or verify a signature

Notice of deficiency   A letter sent by the IRS notifying a taxpayer of the amount of money owed

Notice to show cause   A written document in a lawsuit asking a court to rule on a matter

Objection   A formal protest made by a lawyer in a lawsuit

Offer   The presentment of terms, which, if accepted, may lead to the formation of a contract

Office examination   A tax audit conducted at a regional IRS office

Opinion letter   A written analysis of a client's case prepared by a lawyer

Option   An agreement giving one party the right to choose a certain course of action

Oral contract   An enforceable verbal agreement

Order of execution   A court order enabling a creditor to seize property of a debtor to satisfy a judgment

Pain and suffering   A form of compensable injury

Parol evidence   Oral evidence introduced at a trial to alter or explain the terms of a written contract

Partnership   A voluntary association between two or more competent persons engaged in a business as co-owners for profit

Party   A plaintiff or defendant in a lawsuit

Perjury   Committing false testimony while under oath

Plaintiff   A party who commences a lawsuit

Pleading   A written document that states facts or arguments of a party in a lawsuit

Power of attorney   A document executed by one party authorizing another to act on his or her behalf in specified situations

Pretrial discovery   Legal procedures used to gather information of an opponent before the trial

Private letter ruling   An informal statement provided by the IRS at a taxpayer's request that reflects the IRS's position on a particular issue

Process server   An individual who delivers the summons and/or complaint to the defendant

Product disparagement   False statements or depictions about the quality, condition, or capability of another's product

Product liability   A type of lawsuit arising when a person is injured by a defective product

Promissory note   A written acknowledgment of a debt whereby one party agrees to pay a specified sum on a specified date

Proof   Evidence presented at a trial that is used by a judge or jury to fashion an award

Punitive damages   Money awarded as punishment for a party's wrongful acts

Quantum meruit   A legal principle where a court awards reasonable compensation to a party who performs work, labor, or services at another party's request; also referred to as unjust enrichment

Reasonable reliance   One of the elements required to prove misrepresentation

Rebuttal   The opportunity for a lawyer at a trial to ask his or her client or witness additional questions to clarify points elicited by the opposing lawyer during cross-examination

Release   A written document that, when signed, relinquishes a party's rights to enforce a claim against another

Replevin   A type of lawsuit where one party attempts to recover personal property unlawfully held by another

Reply   A written document in a lawsuit that is the plaintiff's answer to the defendant's counterclaim

Restrictive covenant   A provision in a contract that forbids one party from doing a certain act (e.g., working for another or soliciting customers, etc.)

Retainer   A sum of money paid to a lawyer for services to be rendered

Sales puffery   Statements of a general nature made by a salesperson that the customer is not expected to accept at face value

Service bureau   A company that processes data

Service letter statutes   Laws in some states that require an employer to furnish an employee with written reasons for his or her discharge

Sexual harassment   Prohibited conduct of a sexual nature that occurs in the workplace

Slander   Oral defamation of a party's reputation

Small claims court   A particular court that presides over small disputes (e.g., not exceeding $1,500)

Software   A computer program

Sole proprietorship   An unincorporated business

Statement of fact   Remarks or comments of a specific nature that have a legal effect

Statute   A law created by an administrative body

Statute of frauds   A legal principle requiring certain contracts to be in writing to be enforceable

Statute of limitations   A legal principle that requires a party to commence a lawsuit within a certain period of time

Stipulation   An agreement between lawyers

Subchapter S Corporation   A hybrid corporation having attributes of both a corporation and a partnership

Submission agreement   A signed agreement where both parties agree to submit a present dispute to binding arbitration

Subpoena   A written order demanding a party or witness to appear at a legal proceeding; a subpoena *duces tacum* is a written order demanding a party to bring books and records to the legal proceeding

Summation   The last part of a trial where both lawyers recap the respective positions of their clients

Summons   A written document served upon the defendant that notifies him or her of a lawsuit

Surety   A party who agrees to answer for the debt of another

Tax audit   An IRS investigation of a party's affairs to determine the amount of tax due

Tax court   A particular court that presides over tax disputes

Tax shelter   An entity created to minimize taxes

Testimony   Oral evidence presented by a witness under oath

Time Is of the Essence   A legal expression often included in agreements to specify the requirement of timeliness

Tort   A civil wrong

Trespass   A legal cause of action that arises when one party comes or remains on the property of another without permission

Unfair and deceptive practice   Illegal business and trade acts prohibited by various federal and state laws

Unfair discharge   An employee's termination without legal justification

Verdict   The decision of a judge or jury

Void   Legally without merit

Waiver   A written document that, when signed, relinquishes a party's rights

Warranty   A factual statement made by a seller orally, in writing, by samples, models, etc., regarding the capabilities or qualities of a product or service

Whistle-blowing   Protected conduct where one party complains about the illegal acts of another

Witness   A person who testifies at a judicial proceeding

Worker's compensation   A process where an employee receives compensation for his or her injuries

Index